# No Condemnation!

# No Condemnation!

The Bible and Homosexuality
(A Study Manual)

GARY E. GILTHVEDT

WIPF & STOCK · Eugene, Oregon

Wipf & Stock
An Imprint of Wipf and Stock Publishers
199 W. 8th Ave., Suite 3
Eugene, OR 97401

www.wipfandstock.com

ISBN 13: 978-1-62032-781-4

Manufactured in the U.S.A.

*To My Children's Generation*

*Silently now we would open our hearts to thy presence, which is our hope, and all the beauty of life is its shadow. Teach us thy truth, and grant us to bear ourselves highly in it. Bring us to show mercy, as thou art merciful. So let thy mind be ours, through him who is thy* love to us. Amen.

PAUL SCHERER, *LOVE IS A SPENDTHRIFT*

# Contents

# Abbreviations

BDAG   Walter Bauer, Frederick W. Danker, W. F. Arndt, and F. W. Gingrich. *A Greek–English Lexicon of the New Testament and Other Early Christian Literature*. Second edition. Chicago: University of Chicago Press, 1979

HCSB   *The HarperCollins Study Bible*, edited by Wayne Meeks et al. New York: HarperCollins, 1993

IB   *The Interpreter's Bible*. 12 vols. Edited by George Arthur Buttrick. Nashville: Abingdon, 1952–1969

IDB   *The Interpreter's Dictionary of the Bible*. 4 vols. Edited by George Arthur Buttrick. Nashville: Abingdon, 1962

Int   *Interpretation*

JANT   *The Jewish Annotated New Testament*, edited by Amy-Jill Levine and Marc Zvi Brettler. New York: Oxford, 2011

JSB   *The Jewish Study Bible*, edited by Adele Berlin and Marc Zvi Brettler. New York: Oxford, 2004

JTS   *Journal of Theological Studies*

KJV   *King James Version*

NIB   *The New Interpreter's Bible on CD*. Nashville: Abingdon, 2002

NIV   *The New International Version*

NJPS   TANAKH translation, copyright 1985 by the Jewish Publication Society, Philadelphia

NOAB    *The New Oxford Annotated Bible*, edited by Michael Coogan. New York: Oxford, 2001

NRSV    *New Revised Standard Version*

NTS    *New Testament Studies*

TDNT    *Theological Dictionary of the New Testament.* 10 vols. Edited by Gerhard Kittel and Gerhard Friedrich. Translated by Geoffrey Bromiley. Grand Rapids: Eerdmans, 1964–76

WW    *Word & World*

## ABBREVIATIONS OF SCRIPTURE

### Old Testament

| | | | |
|---|---|---|---|
| Gen | Genesis | Eccl | Ecclesiastes |
| Exod | Exodus | Song | Song of Solomon |
| Lev | Leviticus | Isa | Isaiah |
| Num | Numbers | Jer | Jeremiah |
| Deut | Deuteronomy | Lam | Lamentations |
| Josh | Joshua | Ezek | Ezekiel |
| Judg | Judges | Dan | Daniel |
| Ruth | Ruth | Hos | Hosea |
| 1 Sam | 1 Samuel | Joel | Joel |
| 2 Sam | 2 Samuel | Amos | Amos |
| 1 Kgs | 1 Kings | Obad | Obadiah |
| 2 Kgs | 2 Kings | Jonah | Jonah |
| 1 Chr | 1 Chronicles | Mic | Micah |
| 2 Chr | 2 Chronicles | Nah | Nahum |
| Ezra | Ezra | Hab | Habakkuk |
| Neh | Nehemiah | Zeph | Zephaniah |
| Esth | Esther | Hag | Haggai |
| Job | Job | Zech | Zechariah |
| Ps (pl. Pss) | Psalms | Mal | Malachi |
| Prov | Proverbs | | |

## New Testament

| | | | |
|---|---|---|---|
| *Matt* | *Matthew* | *1 Tim* | *1 Timothy* |
| *Mark* | *Mark* | *2 Tim* | *2 Timothy* |
| *Luke* | *Luke* | *Titus* | *Titus* |
| *John* | *John* | *Phlm* | *Philemon* |
| *Acts* | *Acts* | *Heb* | *Hebrews* |
| *Rom* | *Romans* | *Jas* | *James* |
| *1 Cor* | *1 Corinthians* | *1 Pet* | *1 Peter* |
| *2 Cor* | *2 Corinthians* | *2 Pet* | *2 Peter* |
| *Gal* | *Galatians* | *1 John* | *1 John* |
| *Eph* | *Ephesians* | *2 John* | *2 John* |
| *Phil* | *Philippians* | *3 John* | *3 John* |
| *Col* | *Colossians* | *Jude* | *Jude* |
| *1 Thes* | *1 Thessalonians* | *Rev* | *Revelation* |
| *2 Thes* | *2 Thessalonians* | | |

# Preface

THE APOSTLE ANDREW FOUND himself in places he likely never expected to be. Along with his brother, Simon Peter, he was one of the first twelve followers selected by Jesus. It was a relationship that propelled him beyond the customary, beyond what was known to him, and beyond himself. Tradition tells us that Andrew preached in Asia Minor and Scythia, along the Black Sea, around Kiev and the Volga River, and that he was martyred by crucifixion on an X–shaped cross. Today that symbol is known as the St. Andrew's Cross. Would we surmise that any of this was expected, chosen, or deliberately prepared for, by the apostle whose life we commemorate every November 30?

We who continue in the faith delivered to the saints discover, like Andrew, that we are summoned again and again to think and believe our way amongst challenges for which we had no previous understanding or expectation. Ancient truths have proved uncouth! We may feel hurried to find our truth for our time where our lives are asked to stretch and grow yet again. It is important work, this learning to love what is given to us, and to give what is asked of us.

This importance was once acknowledged to me by a man who had been part of our local church's study on the subject of the Bible and homosexuality. Toward the end of our course he exclaimed, "This is the defining issue of our time!" As a teacher he knew about children. As a husband and father he knew about family. As a Christian he knew about the church. But something strange and new was being asked of him, and somehow he was able to welcome it. Welcoming it, he received courage for exploration. Courageous, he had stability in conversation. Stable, he brings solace to relationships that are given to him.

I believe that this is the path of justice and righteousness. Hundreds of times throughout the Bible the various cognates of a single root find their way into our words *justice, justification, righteousness, righteous.* Even as those terms are all related, so are all persons whom God creates, redeems, and calls to live justly, related as well. In this confidence we have permission, power, and peace: permission for the road that the apostles trod before us and that extends ahead of us, power for the study of the faith laying hold of us, and peace in the connections we share with the entire human family.

GEG
St. Andrew's Day, 2012

# Acknowledgments

WE ARE EACH IN some measure a composite of all the places we have been and the persons we have known. They leave their marks on us in ways both deep and directive. In such light I am grateful for the communities amongst whom I have lived, the churches I have served, and the institutions in which I have taught. The people in those venues have all, in truth, served and taught me.

The closing chapter of my full–time professional life was with the faculty of my college Alma Mater. It was a pleasing experience, not least for the conversations with committed and conscientious colleagues who care about the liberal arts generally and the teaching of religion in particular. It was in one of those conversations, relating to the subject of homosexuality and the Bible, that I remarked about the paucity of resources that focused in a single–minded way on the pertinent biblical texts. Such resources were hard to find, and having said so I thereafter wondered why I shouldn't write one such study myself. What began as an *essay* grew into a *document* and finally is called a *book*.

Throughout this metamorphosis, my wife, Mary consistently affirmed my work and encouraged me to seek its publication. She never wavered in feeling that it was a needed thing in both church and society and that it was a project I could and should do. I am thankful to her and for her.

On those same points Wipf & Stock Publishers seem to have agreed. I am grateful for their offer of publication, the careful and steady steps by which they have led me to the book's final form, and for their commitment to their projects' merit.

My children have each been forthright and honest in their expressions of pleasure at this work and its entering publication. I think of their generation as different from my own in the sense of cautious distance and insightful, healthy skepticism regarding various furnishings in my generation's world. But it is a generation among which many live with a daily, burning sense of justice about the world and its people. I have come to believe they wait for the rest of us to catch on and get there, too. To their generation this book is dedicated.

# 1

## Purpose, Proportion, and Interpretation

THE TITLE OF THIS book, *No Condemnation*, echoes Paul's gospel as proclaimed in Romans 8:1, *There is therefore now no condemnation for those who are in Christ Jesus.* This grand proclamation implies what has gone before in the context of the letter: whereas condemnation lands on sinners through the law, rescue is granted through the work and person of Jesus Christ. This rescue is perfect as to its effect, uninhibited as to its reach, unconditional as to its offer, and productive as to its intent. Thus, we may be confident in the course of the biblical promise and bold in its application to our faith and times.

We may consider the message, *no condemnation*, as the consequence of justification, and its correlation, *in Christ Jesus*, the result of baptism into Christ.[1] *No condemnation in Christ Jesus* is the gospel for all people. It is the ground on which we stand in faith and in study, the path on which we walk in serving the great commission, and the destination of peace and justice that we yearn to reach in this very time.

---

1. Keck, "Romans," 2126.

## PURPOSE AND PERSPECTIVE

The purpose of this book is to encourage faithful conversation about biblical texts that are commonly thought to be about homosexuality. The hope of this book is that text–based reflection in churches about the Bible and homosexuality will contribute to deeper understanding, faithful conversation, and generous demeanor. The first target of this book is pastors and church leaders who want to help their people read and reflect on the timely subject of the Bible and homosexuality. The goal of this book is to serve justice, the prerequisite for peace.

The subject of the Bible and homosexuality is certainly difficult for us in church and society. Tensions between head and heart, between reason and emotion, are often intertwined with the subject. And yet, the needs of our various communities—civil, religious, and familial—overlap on just such a subject. A church can serve its people and simultaneously model for its world how peace and justice flow from the church's sacred writings and vital convictions. The Bible is a ready resource of renewal, a vibrant voice of hope and understanding, and a proven power for compassion and community.

That much conversation about homosexuality has not been conversation at all, but rather successive series of intersecting monologues, shows the need for a different experience of community, church, and society. That address of the subject of homosexuality within both church and society has frequently fallen short of civil propriety and rational proportion proves the need for a more disciplined approach. It could begin among believers. If the heat generated by adversarial approach is inversely proportionate to the light shed on the consideration of our subject, then we will have become shrill about our most tightly held perspectives and we will have eclipsed the calm and sturdy confidence of our one true Shepherd. Here, then, is the need for evangelical reflection and action.

Scripture is our great generative resource of empowerment and guidance. It is common for churches to regard the Bible as the ultimate norm for faith, doctrine, and practice. This regard for sacred writing positions church people to be addressed by the biblical texts that relate, or have been thought to relate, to the subject of homosexuality. Churches can lead by practice and demonstration of careful conversation about ethical norms and faithful action in the light of what the biblical texts say and what they are understood to mean. Churches can model the new creation for a world that is both wearied and worried by its own weakness.

The Bible calls the church to thoughtful deliberation of its message, in the context of respectful conversation, for the sake of implementing its regenerative and redemptive power. Hope in that call exceeds egoism's need to settle a subject by pronouncement. One can state a position in such a way as to preclude exploration or challenge. But it is quite another thing to join a discussion hoping to *contribute to and learn from* the conversation, particularly as the conversation is anchored in Scripture. Thus is community well served.

The conversation about homosexuality *is* needed on every level of human community. We join it here in a simple way and with a specifically chosen means of approach. There are very few biblical texts that herein come directly under our consideration. But it is these texts that are the path on which this study chooses to walk and invite your company.

Our understanding of the subject will remain a work in progress. The scope of the subject, like the breadth and depth of the Bible itself, is bigger, richer, and more generative than any of us can manage. Truth manages us. With that confidence shall hope and charity prevail.

## PROMINENCE AND PROPORTION

There is nothing about homosexuality in the earliest ethical codes of the Hebrews, the Ten Commandments; nothing in the Prophets; nothing in the sayings of Jesus in the four gospels of the New Testament; nothing in the great majority of New Testament

Epistles. Integrity suggests appropriate regard for the fact that, simply put, "*Homosexuality is not a prominent biblical concern.*"[2]

What we can call *the rule of proportion* helps us comprehend the relative importance of a biblical author's particular subject matter as compared or contrasted to other topics within the same written work. By *proportion* is meant the prominence that an author chooses to give a subject in relation to other subjects. What the author includes, emphasizes, excludes, or minimizes helps to disclose the author's purpose and the mission of the written message.

Selectivity thus contributes to the structure and content of a document. Repetition and continuity of subject matter show a proportionate selectivity by which an author serves his or her purpose, seeks to impress the message onto the reader, and sets the subject by sheer weight of ratio in connection to or distance from other ideas or events.[3]

In the case of the Bible and homosexuality, we are dealing with very few texts over all, found in only a few biblical books, and very few mentions within any given biblical book. Thus, when proportion is considered it affirms that homosexuality is not a prominent biblical concern.[4]

But facets of the subject are there. Texts that are usually cited as the most clearly relevant to the subject of homosexuality are from the Old Testament (OT) books of Genesis and Leviticus and the New Testament (NT) letters of Paul. Such references are few and brief, and yet they represent issues that have tremendous impact on our time and culture. These texts deserve and require careful consideration, honest reflection and deliberation, and realistic attribution of importance. Three further points may be added in this regard.

---

2. Furnish, *Teaching*, 53. See Rogers, *Homosexuality*, 69. On the other hand, *poverty* and *the poor* are spoken of thousands of times throughout the Bible. See Wallis, *God's Politics*, 212.

3. Traina, *Bible Study*, 59–63.

4. Furnish, *Teaching*, 53: "As we begin an investigation of the biblical teaching about homosexuality . . . we must keep our sense of proportion. We are not dealing with a fundamental biblical theme. We are not dealing with a major biblical concern."

First, when a subject such as homosexuality is either not mentioned or is referred to only sparsely in Scripture, it can be helpful to our understanding to find analogies in other topics. Are there subjects that share certain characteristics with the subject matter at hand about which an author like Paul or the reported teaching of Jesus or the law and the prophets of the OT have something explicit to say? We may see parallels (of context, content, or conclusions) between our topic and that of another somewhat similar topic or text. The parallel and comparisons themselves can become instructive.[5] Consider, for example, whether the NT message in relation to Gentiles could be a paradigm for the inclusiveness of faith also in relation to homosexuals.

Second, as we think in terms of the wholeness of revelation, Scripture's big picture, and reflect on the dominant message of the Bible, we will notice that not all other aspects of the biblical writings will fit cohesively or neatly into a systematic scheme of thought. Some ideas, in fact, conflict with others and we sometimes have to make choices towards the dominant theme.[6] An example here would be the egalitarian dynamic of Galatians 3:28–29, as over against the demand for subordination in 1 Timothy 2:11–15 or 1 Corinthians 14:34–36.[7] Interpretation includes arbitration, which in turn rests on the core themes of gospel and faith as the standards for grasping the subject.

Third, cultural or societal questions and needs should not govern the meaning of texts but texts can speak to the questions and needs of culture and society. To the extent that it is possible, we can determine what a text meant or was intended to mean when it was written. We can ascertain how throughout the centuries the history of interpretation has acted upon a text and upon our understanding today. It is easy, perhaps natural, for us to assume that

5. Douglas, *Leviticus*, 20–24, speaks of two styles of thought (and two styles of writing) in Leviticus, analogical and rational–instrumental. We could say that this points to comparison as over against analytical explanation.

6. See Dahl, *Paul*, 159–177.

7. Stendahl, *Role of Women*, 28–29.

what we have always thought, what we have been taught, is the real and only truth regarding a portion of Scripture.

But the more we study the Bible the more we find how important it is to study the Bible! New questions arise, new depths of reflection and scholarship occur, and sometimes new understandings of old texts spring forth in surprising ways. One of our quests is to seek after the intention of the text within the context of its writing and conviction of the author. Another of our quests is to apply ourselves to interpretation of the text within the context of our lives today.

It is thus that we often find ourselves challenging our own assumptions about the Bible.[8] We note, for example, that the Apostle Paul makes reference to homosexual activity amidst broader theological arguments relating to more fundamental subjects: idolatry, unbelief, the basis for salvation, and the integrity of the church regarding proclamation and practice. The subject of homosexuality for Paul seems ancillary to or illustrative of broader and bigger issues.

Three questions can help us sort through such issues as addressed by authors like the Apostle Paul. First, what is the main argument, key theme, or central truth that he seeks to establish? We can put this another way: what is the *long* argument, theme, or story, in the context of which a shorter textual episode occurs? Second, if something is what Paul is *for*, then within that argument what is he *against*? And finally, what is the weight of meaning and importance, the appropriate proportion, between the two, between key argument on the one hand, and for/against on the other?

It is not too late in the day to examine our integrity in the relation of proclamation and practice. A keen sense of proportion

8. Brueggemann, *Theology*, 63: "*We now recognize that there is no interest-free interpretation, no interpretation that is not in the service of some interest and in some sense advocacy.* Indeed, it is an illusion of the Enlightenment that advocacy–free interpretation can exist. Interpretation as advocacy is an ongoing process of negotiation, adjudication, and correction. This means, most likely, that there can be no right or ultimate interpretation, but only provisional judgments for which the interpreter is prepared to take practical responsibility, and which must always yet again be submitted to the larger conflictual conversation."

relative to how the Bible speaks of homosexuality and how we think about it is an appropriate place from which to proceed.

## TRANSLATION AND INTERPRETATION

There is another thing to consider about biblical texts before turning to the texts themselves. That has to do with translation. In the translator's move from one language to another, current understandings of a given subject are easily imposed back onto previous eras of history and earlier writings, authors, and believers. The same may be said of today's reader as over against the original author, or today's reader as over against the translator. The spiritual and theological forebears who preceded us may have addressed an aspect of our interest with an understanding of the subject quite different from our own. Consider that there are no words in OT Hebrew or NT Greek equivalent in meaning to our words *homosexual* and *homosexuality*. These modern terms have been imposed backwards from our time onto biblical texts. The impositions are often attended in our understanding by present day meanings that seem to us as exact and timeless renderings of what the texts said or meant at the time the texts were first written.[9]

But in fact, the terms *homosexual* and *homosexuality* did not appear in an English Bible translation until the Revised Standard Version (RSV) of 1946. The terms are not to be found in the King James Version (KJV) of 1611 or in any other English translation prior to 1946. In the 1946 RSV, the word *homosexual* is made to stand for two Greek words in 1 Corinthians 6:9 that are part of a common or standard list of vices about which Paul speaks. Such lists were used for accusation or even insult. In later editions of the RSV New Testament (1971, 1973), the word *homosexual* is dropped in favor of the words *sexual perverts*.[10]

---

9. Scanzoni and Mollenkott, *Neighbor*, 54: "The Bible does not have a great deal to say about homosexuality, and in the original languages the term itself is never used."

10. Furnish, *Teaching*, 54.

Certain questions are in order, the first of which regards techni-cal textual issues. Does our use of words, as well as our understand-ing of their meanings, accurately correspond to what the biblical authors had in mind as best we can tell from the biblical texts them-selves? This question demands help from the larger community of faith. The communion of saints lends head and heart to our under-standing of the Bible in ways of discovery, affirmation, surprise, and correction. Thus, when some recent English translations retain the noun *homosexual* (*The Living Bible,* The New American Standard Version) or the adjective *homosexual perversion* (the New English Bible) or *homosexual perverts* (Today's English Version), we can see that even the linkage of certain terms is telling.

Our second question therefore regards ethics. Is there a jus-tice issue involved in linking together the two words, homosexual and pervert, as well as linking all homosexual persons to the bib-lical condemnations? Some translations (Jerusalem Bible, New American Bible) use *sodomite* or *sodomy* for a male who engages in homosexual activity. The KJV uses *sodomite(s)* in Deut 23:17; 1 Kgs 14:24; 15:12; 22:46; 2 Kgs 23:7. The references are based on Genesis 19 and the men of Sodom, followed by a similar account in Judges 19. But, "It must be emphasized that the development of the sodomitic symbolism sketched above is not in evidence in the Bible itself. Although one may find the word 'sodomite' used in some English versions, even recent ones like the second edition of the RSV New Testament (1 Tim 1:10), the Jerusalem Bible, and the New American Bible, no Hebrew or Greek word formed on the name 'Sodom' ever appears in the biblical manuscripts on which these versions are based."[11]

The emphasis historically on the supposed homosexual as-pect of the Sodom story occurs well after the composition of the Bible, in later non–biblical literature and in the Muslim Qur'an.[12] The emphases of these later writings should be distinct from our study and understanding of biblical texts.

11. Ibid., 57.

12. Rogers, *Homosexuality,* 71.

Our third question regards discretion. How much have problems or modes of translation become problems of theology, faith, and practice on which convictions and assumptions have come to be based today? Later biblical writers (i.e., the prophets, the New Testament) are not preoccupied with the homosexual aspect of the Sodom stories. Sodom is a symbol of God's judgment, the totality of destruction, and the consequences of God's wrath against unbelieving, violent, inhospitable, or greedy people, more than a symbol of homosexual activity: Matt 10:15; Luke 10:12; Matt 11:23–24; Rom 9:29 (Isa 1:9).[13]

Our fourth question is about hermeneutics or interpretation. Has our interpretation and use of the biblical writers' words alienated or distanced the writers' purpose and intention from our discussions today and replaced their intentions with our own? This could be stated another way: have aspects of the culture of our own time been allowed to dominate the use and understanding of biblical texts? Have we shared in and supported assumptions about what the texts first meant that have not only diminished or distracted their message but also added to what some persons have consequently suffered?

Following such lines of inquiry can we allow ourselves to be challenged anew by ancient words that convey the Word that is yet redemptive and renewing?

## EIGHT TEXTS

We will study the biblical texts involved in the discussion about homosexuality as we seek to answer the foregoing questions, deepen our understanding of what the texts say and mean, contribute to our present conversation, and promote just communities. If the biblical texts that actually relate to our subject are in fact few in number, where and what are those texts? Our study focuses on eight passages

13. Isa 1:10–17; 3:9; Jer 23:14; Ezek 16:49; Zeph 2:8–11; Luke 10:10; Jude 7 may refer to the desire for sexual contact of human with heavenly beings; see Scanzoni and Mollenkott, 59.

of Scripture.[14] It is helpful to read each complete passage (cited in parentheses) in its entirety before studying the one or two verses that are the focus of each passage in the material that follows. The eight texts, in the order we will consider them, include: Genesis 19:5 (1–29); Jude 7 (1–25); Judges 19:22–23 (1–30); Leviticus 18:22 (1–30); Leviticus 20:13 (1–27); 1 Timothy 1:9–11 (3–11); 1 Corinthians 6:9–10 (9–17); Romans 1:26–27 (18–32).

We note that four texts are from the Old Testament (OT) books of Genesis and Leviticus, which are among the five books of Moses, or Pentateuch. Thus, they are among the books of the law, what the Hebrew Bible calls *Torah*. The Book of Judges is one of the historical books that immediately follow the Pentateuch in English translations of the OT. The other four texts (Jude, 1 Corinthians, 1 Timothy, and Romans) are among the New Testament (NT) Epistles. They are written for the sake of the lives of the churches and persons whom the authors knew or sought to influence. All eight texts are anchored in the dynamics of their own time and place. They require both our faith and our understanding to render their most authentic help to us today.

We will *not* consider these texts in the order that they occur in the Bible. We will follow Genesis 19 with the NT text from Jude. Jude, although written centuries after Genesis, echoes the Genesis reference to Sodom and Gomorrah. Then we will continue with the Judges 19 story, which in many ways is quite similar to what we find in Genesis 19. The Leviticus texts belong obviously together. We will be somewhat *out of order* again when dealing with the other three NT texts. We will consider 1 Timothy and 1 Corinthians together, because they share common terminology and content. Then we will conclude with Romans, often considered Paul's *magnum opus*, as we converse with Paul's much cited passages in Romans 1.

14. Rogers, 69: "None of these texts is about Jesus, nor do they include any of his words."

# 2

# The Broken Community

*Genesis 19:1–29*

THE TWO TEXTS THAT come simultaneously to our attention, from Genesis 19 and Judges 19, are representative of the importance to their time and culture of the gift and practice of hospitality. The act of receiving, protecting, and providing for the sojourner as a guest was a necessary civility on which the provider knew he might someday himself be dependent. Throughout the Mediterranean world, hospitality was regarded as a sacred duty and its challenge was more steadfastly kept than many written laws. Even an enemy would be protected as a guest. The host expressed his righteousness with his providence of food, water, and care for the guest and even for the guest's animals.[1]

Jesus was dependent on hospitality for his daily needs, care, and lodging. The same civility was assumed for the care of his apostles and to a considerable extent was responsible for the extensive journeys of the early Christian missionaries. "Hospitality was the chief bond which brought the churches a sense of unity."[2]

1. Kooy, "Hospitality," 654. See Gen 18:1–8; 19:1–11; 24:14–61; Rogers, 70.
2. Kooy, 654. See Matt 8:20; 9:10; Mark7:24; 14:3; Luke 7:36; 8:3; 9:52;

The bond of hospitality continued beyond the period of the New Testament and indeed played a significant part in the growth and expansion of the Christian Church. The historian and dogmatician, Adolf von Harnack, wrote extensively of the practice of hospitality in the churches of early Christianity. The practice took the direction of care and support generally for the vulnerable and dispossessed. Harnack refers to three examples of early Christian writing that witness to the pervasiveness of hospitality throughout the mission and ministry of early churches.

First, Harnack refers to Clement, who cites a letter from the Roman to the Corinthian church (AD 96), as Clement describes what it means to be a church: "Who did not proclaim the splendid style of your *hospitality?* . . . Thus, a profound and unsullied peace was bestowed on all, with *an insatiable craving for beneficence.*"[3]

Second, Harnack refers to Justin's *Apology* (lxvii), in which Justin concludes his description of true Christian worship with references to generosity, charity, and hospitality for the aid of, ". . . orphans, widows, those who are in want owing to sickness or any other cause, those who are in prison, and strangers who are on a journey."[4]

Third, Harnack refers to Tertullian's *Apology* (xxxix), who speaks of the churches' giving of funds, "deposits of piety . . . expended upon . . . feeding and burying poor people, on behalf of boys and girls who have neither parents nor money, in support of old folk unable now to go about, as well as for people who are shipwrecked, or who may be in the mines or exiled in islands or in prison . . ."[5]

Thus, from the Old Testament, through the New, and into the history and expansion of the church, the practice of hospitality has been integral to the mission of the faithful. It indicates the

---

10:38: 14:1; John 12:2 regarding Jesus. See Acts 16:15; 18:27: 3 John 5–6 regarding those sent out. See Rom 15:26–27; 2 Cor 9:1–2; Phil 4:10, 14–18 regarding churches and this Christian tradition.

3. Harnack, *Expansion*, 188, cites 1 Clement i, ii. Harnack's third chapter ("The Gospel of Love and Charity") relates to the social emphasis of the church in its period of early expansion. See his, *What Is Christianity?*, 88–101.

4. Harnack, *Expansion*, 189.

5. Ibid., 190.

covenant life as taught by the law and prophets, the ethics of the kingdom as preached and exemplified by Jesus, the new humanity as witnessed and asserted by the Apostle Paul, and the alternative society known as the church, whose mission was from the beginning aimed at helping those who could not help themselves.

As we enter our texts in Genesis 19 and Judges 19, we see the importance of the practice of hospitality for the well-being of its beneficiaries and the good of a community, and the devastating consequences when the standard of hospitality is not achieved by those who are in the position to provide it.

The two texts from Genesis 19 and Judges 19 share proximity in our study due to their similarity: travelers in a strange city, rude and violent citizens demanding access to violate or humiliate the male visitors, and the intention or execution of rape. But each text has its own persons and plot which, in the case of Genesis, includes Lot, Abraham's nephew.[6]

It is to be remembered, furthermore, that in the case of the Genesis text we are dealing with only a part of the long-range story. The promise given to Abraham (12:1–3) is transmitted, by divine designation, to Abraham's son, Isaac, and thereafter to the twelve tribes of Israel. Along the way, there are perils that could undermine the promise and the covenant relationship. There are dangers that could make folly of what God had sworn to accomplish. But neither danger nor peril prevails. But it is one such danger of which we read in Genesis 19.[7]

---

6. Fretheim, "Genesis," 322, reminds us that Lot is part of Abraham's journey of faith. Rosenberg, "Genesis," 3, identifies the major movements or sections of Genesis: Primary History (chs. 1–11); Abraham (12:1—25:18); Jacob (25:19—36:43); Joseph and his brothers (37–50).

7. Carr, "Genesis," 10, ". . . the book of Genesis has proven its ability to speak to people of varying cultures and times. It is not just a story about things happening in a bygone age. It is a crystallization of Israel's most fervent beliefs and hopes as expressed in genealogy and vivid narrative."

No Condemnation!

## GENESIS 19:5 (1–29)

Genesis 19 tells the story of Lot hosting two messenger–visitors in his home in the city of Sodom. The visitors had come from their stay with Abraham and Sarah (ch. 18). Lot also practices the standard hospitality as a service and a protection for guests. Such hospitality was not merely a nice courtesy, but was rather a demanding and perilous provision and protection.[8] Hospitality provided for the needs of the guests and granted protection from the elements and from crime or danger, contributing not only to individual well–being, but that of society as well. "The people of Sodom show no sign of what hospitality entails at all."[9] The crisis arises after the evening meal, before the guests retire for the night, when the men of the city surrounded the house. We make several observations.

First, we note that every male of the city was present. Remember that no terminology referring to *homosexual, homosexuality,* or *sodomy* occurs in this text. And yet the text is commonly seen as a story about how God destroyed the city and its people because of displeasure with the male inhabitants' homosexuality. But it is not credible to think that every last man, young and old—every father, son, or husband—was a homosexual, for then there would have been no continuing population in the city of Sodom. Sodom is not depicted as a gay community.[10]

Second, we note also the use of the verb *to know* for what the mob wants to perpetrate onto the guests. This verb is used hundreds of times throughout the Hebrew Scriptures but only very few times does it refer to sexual knowing.[11] In this case it is clear that the objective of the mob of men was not simply sexual.[12]

8. Brueggemann, *Genesis,* 164.

9. Fretheim, "Genesis," 474.

10. Scanzoni and Mollenkott, 54–56.

11. Nissinen, *Homoeroticism,* 46, says that "the verb indisputably signifies sexual 'knowing' only in about a dozen of its almost one thousand occurrences." Rogers, 71, points out that the verb is never used in connection with homosexual acts.

12. Brueggemann, *Genesis,* 164: "The use of the term 'outcry' in 18:20–21; 19:13 argues in the direction of a general abuse of justice."

That is, the intention clearly was not romantic or loving sexual activity.[13] It was about violent domination and humiliation.[14] The plan was to perpetrate what today we would call a sex *crime*. The mob was xenophobic, having to exert domination, even in violent and abusive ways, over those presumed to be enemies, in order to disgrace them, put them in their place, and preserve the power of control of home territory. "Foreigners are clearly not welcome."[15]

Third, we note as well that Lot held so tenaciously to protecting his visitors that he offered his own virgin daughters to the mob in lieu of mob harm to his male guests.[16] Does the text seem to commend Lot for this sacrifice in view of his commitment to the sacred trust of hospitality?[17] The result for the daughters could have been fatal; the cost certainly would have been extraordinary. Coincidentally it would have diminished Lot as well, in view of the shame that accrued to a father whose daughters' virginity had been disgraced (Deut 22:20–21). The men of Sodom showed contempt for this degree of hospitality in Lot, even as they had ignored and transgressed its requirements relative to visitors in their community.[18]

13. Wink, *Homosexuality*, 1: "Their brutal behavior has nothing to do with the problem of whether genuine love expressed between consenting adults of the same sex is legitimate or not."

14. Furnish, *Teaching*, 54; Rogers, 70.

15. Rogers, 70; Brueggemann, *Genesis*, 164: ". . . the Bible gives considerable evidence that the sin of Sodom was not specifically sexual, but a general disorder of a society organized against God. Thus in Isa 1:10; 3:9, the reference is to injustice; in Jer 23:14, to a variety of irresponsible acts which are named; and in Ezek 16:49 the sin is pride, excessive food, and indifference to the needy." The word, *xenophobic*, refers to fear, hatred, or mistrust of those different from oneself. They are the others, the outsiders. See Nissinen, 46–47.

16. Rogers, 71: "The hosts do not seem to think of the attackers as primarily homosexual, or they would not offer women for them to abuse."

17. Fretheim, "Genesis," 473, indicates that according to ch. 19 Lot seems to have taken on some of the qualities of his environment in Sodom.

18. Nissinen, 48: "Abraham's (18:1–5) and Lot's (19:1–3) exemplary hospitality are the opposite of the outrageous behavior of the Sodomites. This is the background for understanding the Sodomite men's rape attempt. (It is) phallic aggression generated by xenophobic arrogance."

Fourth, we note the attitude of the mob to Lot himself as an outsider who tries to reason or bargain with them (v. 9): "This fellow came here as an alien, and he would play the judge! Now we will deal worse with you than with them." Their motivation was, "to show their supremacy and power over the guests—and ultimately over Lot himself, a resident alien to whom a lesson was to be taught about the place of a foreigner in the city of Sodom. Lot's daughters, therefore, were not a satisfactory substitute."[19]

Finally, we note the importance of the fact that Lot's male visitors were angels (19:1). The Lord, together with two divine attendants, had visited Abraham, (18:1–2), before two of them moved onwards to the city of Sodom (18:16). It is these two angels who were in Lot's home when the violent mob approached Lot's house. The angels' mission had been previously decided: to destroy Sodom as punishment for its evil and in response to its outrageous reputation. Sodom's evil was about to be perpetrated against Lot's angel visitors.

This was not the first time that such trouble was brewing between heaven and earth, between divine and human realms. In Genesis 6 we are told that *the sons of God* were attracted to human women, took them sexually, and bore children with them (6:1–4). Verse 5 immediately follows with the commentary about the widespread wickedness of humankind, God's sorrow over having made them (v. 6), and the decision (v. 7) to blot out all living creatures.

Knust says of this text in Genesis 6: ". . . the episode of the 'sons of God' who had intercourse with human women could only mean one thing: angels had breached the divine realm in order to sate their illicit sexual desires. Genesis 6, elaborated and expanded in other writings, became a principal explanation for the introduction of evil into the world."[20]

---

19. Ibid., 49.

20. Knust, *Unprotected Texts*, 155. The other writings to which she refers (156) include 1 Enoch (not a canonical book but among the Dead Sea Scrolls) in which ". . . new explanations for the bad behavior of angels were developed, pointing out just how devastating the consequences of angelic lust could be." The importance of this relates to divine–human boundaries. So also 2 Baruch, a writing from the second century CE, speaks in equally negative

In Genesis 6 the story is of angels' lust for human women. In Genesis 19, the story is of human lust for angels. In both cases the divine–human boundary is crossed, God's harmonious order is perverted, God's sovereignty is threatened by both heaven and earth, and God must stand in authority over against both realms.[21] Then, covenant communities are accordingly warned of the potential danger of subjection to angelic passion and contact. Paul's enigmatic comment about angels in 1 Cor 11:10, protection against which may include the need for women to cover their heads, could be understood this way. Jude 6–7 alludes to the angels "who did not keep their own rule but left their dwelling . . . indulged in fornication and went after strange flesh . . ." as had the men of Sodom and Gomorrah.[22]

Had the mob of Genesis 19 succeeded in its objective to humiliate and dominate the sojourners to whom hospitality was due, it would have been a success implemented by the weapon of rape.[23] "Rape is not a sexual act so much as it is an act of violence."[24] Heterosexual rape shows a man's disdain for and domination of a woman. Homosexual rape is a way for the conqueror to flaunt victory over enemies or superiority over the *other* by treating the conquered with the greatest possible contempt, forcing on them the passive role of a woman in (anal) intercourse. Because women were thought to be inferior, therefore to be treated as a woman was to be inferior.[25] The result is dominance, subjugation, and humiliation.

There is no signal of erotic attraction in Genesis 19, but only the ugly desire to disgrace and diminish the outsider and stranger.

---

and judgmental language of the mingling of angels with human women. Knust says, "In other words, sex with angels leads inexorably to divine punishment."

21. Brueggemann, *Genesis*, 72, "The perversion wrought by the sons of God and the daughters of men is another example of the attempt to 'be like God.' And so the intervention of God (v. 3) is for the sake of his sovereignty."

22. Knust, 159–162.

23. Fretheim, "Genesis," 474: "If the assault had succeeded, the result could only be described as gang rape . . . but one example of Sodom's sins . . . we trivialize the narrative if we focus on this one sin."

24. Scanzoni and Mollenkott, 56.

25. Rogers, 70.

Just as the men of Sodom were belligerent and aggressive from the outset, so the entire episode portrays the antithesis of hospitality and breakdown of civil society. Fretheim comments, "The text . . . is the most frequently cited Genesis passage in the rest of the Bible. Sodom and Gomorrah become a conventional image for heinous sins and severe disaster. Apparently these cities symbolize the worst that can be imagined. The nature of Sodom's sins may vary, but the mistreatment of other human beings tops the list; inhospitality lends itself to diverse development (Jer 23:14). Later texts recall Sodom's judgment, even its specific form (see Ps 11:6; Ezek 38:22; Rev 21:8)."[26]

"The most frequently cited Genesis passage," yes, but the citations are not to reinforce accusations against the sin of *sodomy* (a word the Bible never uses). None of the OT texts that refer to the cities of Sodom and Gomorrah do so for the sake of speaking against sexual immorality, much less homosexual activity. The cities are cited as extreme examples of injustice, cruelty, and greed. Thus, Knust says,

> Though the Bible knows nothing of this later identification of Sodom with sex between men, the story was cited for other reasons. The prophets of Israel . . . regarded Sodom's misdeeds as economic, not sexual: from their perspective, God destroyed Sodom and Gomorrah because the people had become selfish and corrupt, not because they were sexually depraved. Thus, in an oracle condemning Judah's rulers, the prophet Isaiah compared the men of Judah to the rulers of Sodom, arguing that God's punishment necessarily descends upon those who mistreat widows and orphans: *Hear the word of the LORD, you rulers of Sodom! Listen to the teaching of our God, you people of Gomorrah! What to me is the multitude of your sacrifices? says the LORD . . . Wash yourselves: make yourselves clean; remove the evil of your doings from before my eyes; cease to do evil, learn to do good; seek justice, rescue the oppressed, defend the orphan, plead for the widow. (Isa 1:10–11, 16–17; compare Isa. 3:9)* In other words, to

26. Fretheim, "Genesis," 473.

Isaiah the Sodom incident proves that injustice against the poor leads inexorably to divine punishment, a sentiment repeated by the prophet Ezekiel some time later.[27]

Abraham's faith is the antithesis to Sodom's violence. Hospitality witnesses to a greater framework within which it belongs. In Genesis 12–25 that framework is covenant righteousness. Abraham had been chosen for a life of *doing righteousness and justice* (18:19). Over against this call was the grave sin of Sodom and Gomorrah (18:20), and the failure to locate even ten righteous persons from within their citizenry (18:32). Abraham's righteous justice intercedes and prays for the very people who have none of it. He boldly reminds God (18:25), "Shall not the Judge of all the earth do what is just?" Fifty righteous, forty–five, thirty, twenty, ten—such are the intercessions of covenant faith as Abraham prays for the *others*. Conversely, it was the *others* for whom the men of Sodom showed disdain and plotted abuse.[28] Those who plotted the destruction of *others* received destruction. The one who interceded for *others'* rescue was given rescue. Intercession serves call (12:2–3): "I will bless you . . . you will be a blessing." The story commences toward its outcome as Abraham's visitors set out from his tent and they "looked toward Sodom" (18:16).[29] Abraham righteously argues for blessing. But for Sodom it was not to be.[30]

---

27. Knust, 166.

28. Brueggemann, *Genesis*, 162–177.

29. The NRSV translates הַמַּלְאָכִים *(hammal'ākîm)* as "the angels" (19:1, 15). The singular word in Hebrew (מַלְאָךְ) means *messenger*. See Gen 16:7; 21:17; 22:11; Exod 3:2; 14:19; 23:20 for angel/messenger.

30. Fretheim, "Genesis," 474, "His (*sic* Lot's) daughters were betrothed (v. 14); Israel condemned to death those who rape betrothed women (Deut 22:23–24). Threatened sexual abuse and violence, both homosexual and heterosexual, constitutes sufficient evidence to move forward with judgment."

# 3

## Honor and Shame

*Jude 1–25*

JUDE, THE SECOND-TO-LAST BOOK of the Bible, is one chapter in length. It is attributed to Jude, the brother of both Jesus (Mark 6:3) and James (Jude 1). We do not know to what faith communities the letter was originally sent or the exact time of its sending. Jude could be one of the earliest writings in the New Testament. The letter is one of the few to derive from Palestinian Christianity. It is also quite plausible that Jude, the brother of Jesus, was in fact the letter's author. Paul refers to *the brothers of the Lord* (1 Cor 9:5) as married, traveling, supported apostles, among whom Jude would have been included.[1]

---

1. Bauckham, "Jude," 2304–5; Brosend, "Rhetoric," 292–305. Bauckham accepts the plausibility of an early date for Jude, and Brosend sees no strong reason to reject authorship by Jesus' brother and would place the writing of the letter earlier than the destruction of the Temple in 70 CE (294). But see Reicke, *Jude*, 190–191, who suggests that Jude and its parallel material in 2 Peter 2 may both have drawn on a similar (oral?) tradition, addressed to Jewish Christians, and Jude, if not written by the brother of Jesus and James, would have been written "in the spirit of his mentor" in the last decades of the first century.

Jude writes to warn of God's impending judgment against immorality, to encourage practical living of the gospel with faith, hope, and love, and to advise against leaders who claim that their spirituality exempts them from every form of moral authority. Jude 7 is the key verse for our purposes: "Likewise Sodom and Gomorrah and the surrounding cities, which, in the same manner as they, indulged in sexual immorality and pursued unnatural lust, serve as an example by undergoing a punishment of eternal fire."

This mention of the two notorious cities is the third in a group of three references to specific traditions. We note: Jude 5 refers to the deliverance out of Egypt and subsequent destruction of those who did not believe; Jude 6 refers to angels who did not keep their proper place and relationships and thus suffer captivity and judgment; Jude 7 refers to Sodom and Gomorrah, sexual immorality, unnatural lust, and eternal punishment by fire. These references are directed against "intruders (who) have stolen in among you, people who long ago were designated for this condemnation." They are ungodly; they pervert the grace of God; they deny Christ (v. 4).

Jude is clear about the inseparability of faith in the Christian gospel and moral obedience to Christ. The proponents of the teaching against which he militates taught that visionary spirituality gave them license to disregard moral authority (v. 8); God's grace gave them license to do as they please (v. 4); what they pleased was sexual indulgence and unnatural lust (v. 7).[2] Despite the fact that the two cities are considered the epitome of wickedness, Jude is alone among the biblical writings explicitly to relate the sin of Sodom and Gomorrah to sexual immorality.[3] Should we assume that this refers to homosexuality? The letter indicates three aspects of a more likely understanding.[4]

2. Bauckham, "Jude," 2304.

3. Rogers, 75; Bauckham, *Jude*, 53, "Σόδομα και Γόμορρα, 'Sodom and Gomorrah,' had long been regarded as the paradigm case of divine judgment (Deut 29:23; Isa 1:9; 13:19; Jer 23:14; 49:18; 50:40; Lam 4:6; Hos 11:8; Amos 4:11; Zeph 2:9)."

4. Bauckham, *Jude*, 54, "In Jewish tradition the sin of Sodom was rarely specified as homosexual practice . . . The incident with the angels is usually treated as a violation of hospitality, and the Sodomites are condemned

First, Jude 6 refers to angels, likely of Gen 6:1–4, who *did not keep their own position, but left their proper dwelling,* and having come down to earth had sexual relations with the daughters of humankind. The renegade angels recognized no border between heaven and earth, between divine and human realms. The Genesis passage is a prelude to the story of Noah that immediately follows, after the explanation that the inclination of human hearts was constantly evil and its effects cosmically pervasive. And yet in Jude 6, "The sin of the angels is not described as engaging in forbidden relations with humans, but as not keeping 'their own position' and leaving 'their proper dwelling.'"[5] That is, the angels transgressed the human–divine boundary, thus producing the Nephilim (6:4). What immediately follows in the Genesis 6 account is the report of wickedness so widespread (6:5) and intolerable that God responds with the sorrowful decision to blot out all living creatures (6:12–13). The breaching of the boundary between the divine and human realms was itself an invitation to God's wrath.[6]

Second, Jude 7 continues with a comparison, *likewise,* and *in the same manner as they,* referring to the renegade angels and their example as followed by Sodom and Gomorrah. The lust of the men of those cities, Gen 19:1, 4–5 reminds us, was a lust for the *angels* who had visited Lot and his household. The men of the cities violated angelic–human boundaries. Just as the angels of Jude 6 had done, so also the men of Sodom and Gomorrah did not keep

---

especially for their hatred of strangers . . . their pride and affluence . . . their sexual immorality in general . . . Jude's intention in stressing here the peculiar sexual offenses of both the Watchers and the Sodomites is probably to highlight the shocking character of the false teachers' violation of God–given order."

5. Brosend, "Rhetoric," 297.

6. Knust, 155. Fretheim, "Genesis," 383, points out that the "taking" of women implies abuse. This breach of divine boundaries in Genesis 6 impacts also the Sodom episode in Genesis 19. Knust, 162, continues, ". . . the sin of the Sodomites was horrific not because the men of Sodom sought to rape *men* but because they wanted to rape *angels.*"

their position but left their proper dwelling and, not knowing their place, went after *strange flesh*.[7]

Third, Jude 8 refers to the *glorious ones* (a common term for angels) who were slandered by those against whom Jude writes. These dangerously licentious slanderers have claimed freedom from the same moral order of which the angels were the guardians. This claim and their consequent behavior have disparaged the angels and the order they guard. Consequently, the Lord's judgment follows, to which Michael the archangel consigns the offenders (v. 9).[8] It is telling that immediately before the mention in Jude 8 of the *glorious ones* the opponents are charged with the accusation that they *reject authority*.[9]

Does this connect to how the letter opens, with the signature of *a servant of Jesus Christ and brother of James*? Whose authority is it that the intruders reject?

> One assumes it is the authority of the author that is being challenged, authority derived not from being among the apostles of v. 17 but by virtue of being Christ's servant and James's (*sic*) brother, and, so well known within the

---

7. Bauckham, *Jude*, 54: "τὸν ὅμοιον τρόπον τούτοις ἐκπορνεύσασαι καὶ ἀπελθοῦσαι ὀπίσω σαρκὸς ἑτέρας, (*ton homoion tropon toutois ekporneusasai kai apelthousai opiso sarkos heteras*) 'which practiced immorality in the same way as the angels and hankered after strange flesh.' The second clause explains the first. As the angels fell because of their lust for women, so the Sodomites desired sexual relations with angels. The reference is to the incident in Gen 19:4–11. σαρκὸς ἑτέρας (*sarkos heteras* ) 'strange flesh,' cannot, as many commentators and most translations assume, refer to homosexual practice, in which the flesh is not 'different' (ἑτέρας); it must mean the flesh of angels. The sin of the Sodomites . . . reached its zenith in this most extravagant of sexual aberrations, which would have transgressed the order of creation as shockingly as the fallen angels did." Bauckham, 43, points out that a similar phrase occurs in Judg 2:12 (LXX), where Israel abandons its true God for going after the Baals. See Rogers, 75: Jude 7 seems to draw "a parallel between the 'unnatural lust' of angels who wanted to have sex with human women (Gen 6:1–4) and the men of Sodom who wanted to have sex with (male) angels (Gen 19:1–29)."

8. Bauckham, "Jude," 2305–6.

9. Bauckham, *Jude*, 11, identifies the opponents as itinerant charismatics of an antinomian nature who portrayed the grace (of God in Christ) as delivering them from all moral constraint.

community it need not be mentioned, a brother of the Lord. The reference to Jesus as 'our only Master and Lord'... indicates the level of authority derived from this identification. In rejecting the author's authority, the opponents deny Christ.[10]

This is a key to the context as well as to the content. The issue is honor and shame:

Indeed, honor might be considered the pivotal value of the Mediterranean world . . . . Primarily, honor derives from one's clan, family, and father . . . Honor accrues to one's family name, and all family members share in it when it is publicly acknowledged and respected . . . When one member is honored, all are honored; but when one is shamed, the group shares this loss.[11]

There is a pattern to exchanges in which honor is at stake and shame is to be turned away. The pattern has four standard elements: (1) a claim to honor or precedence, (2) a challenge to that claim, (3) a riposte or retort to the challenge, (4) a public verdict. "But the key to this interaction is the public nature of the dispute and public acknowledgment or denial of respect."[12]

Jude would thus be responding not only as a holder of what he considers the true faith but also as a member of Jesus' family. This is the source of Jude's authority and hence the need to respond to those who have challenged, shamed, or denied that family and that authority. Jude indicates and names this denial in v. 4. Furthermore, the denial, shaming, and turning away from the truth amount to pollution. Three things are involved here.

First, purity is dependent on the usual order of life within a structured and classified whole. Persons are socialized from birth to know what is in place or out of place and how a thing or a person is either pure and clean or polluted and unclean, depending on

---

10. Brosend, "Rhetoric," 302.

11. Jerome Neyrey, *Jude*, 3–4.

12 Ibid., 5. See Malina, *Cultural Anthropology*, 25–7.

whether it or one is in place or out of place. To be out of place is to be in violation of common and assumed order and propriety.[13]

Second, purity and pollution relate to entrance and exit. Belonging grants proper entrance. Entrance pollutes if there is no belonging for the entrant. One who enters without belonging is out of place, pollutes the groups, and subverts the tradition. They are deviants and they are dangerous.[14]

Third, it is precisely such issues about which Jude warns: certain intruders have stolen in; they pervert the grace of our God; they deny our only Master. The intrusion of *illegal* entrants involves dishonoring Jesus Christ with denial and licentiousness (v. 4).[15] Jude cites three examples of those who did not keep their place, who fell from grace, and who caused pollution with them. These included the Exodus generation who despite deliverance did not believe (Num 14:20-3), the angels of Gen 6:1-4, and the cities of Sodom and Gomorrah (Genesis 19).

In exactly the same ways, the adversaries against whom Jude writes have *blasphemed* against the *glorious ones* (v. 8). The insult of blasphemy is a challenge to role, status, honor, and authority.[16] The strident accusations in v. 4 are followed by an exhaustive list of denigrations in vv. 8-16. The list more than criticizes the opponents: it demonizes them (v. 9) as worthy of condemnation.

It may seem that readers are thus faced with the alternatives of either, (1) castigating the condemned and consigning them to eternal punishment so as to preserve believers' moral purity, or (2) acknowledging the author's attack as mean-spirited, unworthy of the faith in whose name it is written, a negation of Christian humility and going on the attack at precisely the points where Christ himself would have turned the other cheek.[17]

It is not unusual for interpreters to consider the letter of Jude as an example of rhetorical overkill. It is helpful, however, to

---

13. Neyrey, *Jude*, 10-11.

14. Ibid., 53.

15. Ibid., 59.

16. Ibid., 69, 197.

17. Brosend, "Rhetoric," 304.

remember that there was a poignant and urgent expectation of the immanent end-time in Jude's day (as we see also in Paul). This put believers like Jude of a mind to see themselves as living on the cusp of the age to come and with the conviction that the time in which they lived was the fulfillment of what God had promised to do and was now doing. In such a time it was crucial to contend for the faith.[18] Furthermore, it is helpful for us to notice four things that moderate the usual judgment about Jude's *excess.*

First, the usual view exaggerates the relative importance of the polemical section of Jude 4–19 and does not sufficiently notice the positive material in 1–2, 24–5, in forms of blessing and benediction.

Second, the usual view tends to ignore how the polemical material is not mere denunciation, but rather names ethical libertinism as that of sinners of the last days, the judgment of whom was prophesied in Scripture and in apostolic teaching.

Third, the usual view slights the fact that the polemical material in vv. 4–19 hinges entirely on ethical libertinism as behavior incurring God's judgment. "The controversy is about the moral implications of the Christian Gospel."[19]

Fourth, the usual view does not sufficiently notice that the polemical section is not addressed to Jude's opponents. It intends to persuade Jude's *readers* of their danger; it is characteristic of early Jewish Christian apocalyptic material and God's intervention in history to set things right.

Jude (3) found it "necessary to write and appeal to you to contend for the faith." His contention was his proclamation. It is important for the church today to recognize that the *rhetoric of argumentation* is different from the *rhetoric of proclamation,* and that difference "must be accounted for in our readings."[20] But that difference must also be accounted for within our witness to the cultures and societies of our time, wherein the rhetoric of argumentation is

18. Bauckham, *Relatives of Jesus,* 152, understands Jude as resembling "eschatological prophecy which the interpreter applies to the events of his own time, understood as the time of eschatological fulfillment."

19. Ibid., 156; for the four points summarized here see 152–6.

20. Brosend, "Rhetoric" 304.

too often bereft of proclamation. It is there that the church meets the test of witnessing to and living as a working model of God's order, ". . . the essential structure of spiritual reality, which has its source in God and whose development is determined by the will of God."[21]

## Summary

We are involved with the question of the authority of Scripture. It is an authority not merely of letter but of Spirit, not only of words but of Person. The Savior rules the Scriptures. He is the Scriptures' content and he is the content's standard. This very thought was articulated a century ago by a faithful preacher and theologian of the cross, P. T. Forsyth. He convincingly said,

> The Bible's inspiration, and its infallibility, are such as pertain to redemption and not theology, to salvation and not mere history. It is as infallible as a Gospel requires, not as a system. Remember that Christ did not come to bring a Bible but to bring a Gospel. The Bible arose afterwards from the Gospel to serve the Gospel. We do not treat the Bible aright, we do not treat it with the respect it asks for itself, when we treat it as a theologian, but only when we treat it as an apostle, as a preacher, as the preacher in the perpetual pulpit of the Church. It is saturated with dogma, but its writers were not dogmatists; and it concerns a Church, but they were not ecclesiastics. The Bible, the preacher, and the Church are all made by the same thing—the Gospel. The Gospel was there before the Bible, and it created the Bible, as it creates the true preacher and the true sermon everywhere. And it is for the sake and service of the Gospel that both Bible and preacher exist. We are bound to use both, at any cost to tradition, in the way that gives freest course to the Gospel in which they arose.[22]

---

21. Mackay, *God's Order*, ix.

22. Forsyth, *Positive Preaching*, 15. The book is based on the Lyman Beecher Lectures on Preaching, given at Yale University in 1907.

No Condemnation!

Jude's *rhetoric of proclamation* would rescue from sin by forcefully naming it, but also naming the Name that is above every name. The rhetoric of proclamation finally is anchored in God's action in Christ for the rescue of all humankind. This proclamation of rescue can, as in Jude, be transmitted even by way of exhortation (Jude 21–2): "Keep yourselves in the love of God; look forward to the mercy of our Lord Jesus Christ that leads to eternal life. And have mercy on some who are wavering."

# 4

## The Anarchy of Violence

*Judges 19:1–30*

THE ENTIRE PASSAGE OF Judges 19:1–30 is the first of three con-
secutive parts that relate to traditions about the Tribe of Benjamin.
The three parts comprise three chapters in the Book of Judges: (1)
19:1–30 is about the horrific abuse, rape, and murder of the concubine; (2) 20:1–48 is about the war against the tribe of Benjamin
by the other tribes of Israel in response to the Gibeah incident;
(3) 21:1–24 is about the procuring of wives for the survivors of
Benjamin after the war that had all but wiped out the tribe. The last
verse of the last chapter (21:25) is the final reminder of how such
disastrous events have ensued: *there was no king in Israel.*[1]

The opening words of Judges 19 echo a message that has also
been sounded earlier: *In those days, when there was no king in Israel
. . .* This theme appears in 17:6 and 18:1, as well as 19:1, and finally
in 21:25. The first and last of these citations describe the ungoverned
situation's consequence: *all the people did what was right in their own*

---

1. Trible, "Violence," 65, identifies the segments of ch. 19: introduction
(1–2); two scenes (3–10; 15b–28); interlude (11–15a); conclusion (29–30).

*eyes*. "The refrain builds an expectation that chaos, disorder, and disobedience will characterize the stories that follow."[2]

The repetition of the refrain is instructive: insufficient government accounts for the wantonness in the land, shows need for rule, and prepares for acceptance of that rule by monarchy. "The condition of anarchy called for change, and soon a prophet was born in the hills of Ephraim, Samuel (1 Samuel 1), who restored order and prepared the way for the first king of Israel, Saul (1 Sam. 8–12)."[3]

But the land was yet without a king and, as the story testifies, lawless as well. People found only within themselves what level of order and ethical standard would motivate their course of action. Law and king would not, could not, be consulted. "The lack of a king is a license for anarchy and violence."[4] This ominous situation of anarchy, vulnerable to opportunism and exploitation, exacerbated ". . . Israel's dysfunctional confession of the Lord's sovereignty and governance by covenantal ethic."[5] Israel thus lacked conscientious adherence to covenant life and had neither will nor ability to give voice to covenant identity. Indeed, chaos, disorder, and disobedience follow, along with violence and murder.

Women are central to the themes of Judges, with key roles in the stories that unfold. They are leaders (Deborah, 4:4), heroines (Jael, 4:21), and victims (Jephthah's daughter, 11:34; the concubine of ch. 19). The pervasiveness of violence attaches to the presence of these women.[6] Beyond the actions of the female characters in Judges, women serve as a metaphor for Israel itself.[7] Their treatment indicates the health and faithfulness of the covenant people.

2. Olson, "Judges," 875.

3. Nissinen, 51.

4. Trible, 84.

5. Boling, "Judges," 401.

6. Hackett, "Women's Lives," 356–364, says that violence in the Book of Judges is a function of the lawless era it describes and is also intertwined with the lives of women.

7. Ibid., 364, "The complex interweaving of these stories throughout the book of Judges argues for an underlying system of meaning that sees in women's bodies a substitute for a unified Israel."

Dennis Olson speaks of this relationship between Israel's faithfulness and the treatment of women:

> It has been noted throughout the book of Judges that the changing power relationships, independence, and treatment of the many women characters in the book function as benchmarks for the health and faithfulness of God's people. Early on in the judges' era, women like Achsah (1:11–15), Deborah (4:4–10), and Jael (4:17–22) displayed glimpses of boldness, leadership, and power as subjects of their destinies in the midst of a largely patriarchal context. Israel seemed to function more effectively as a religious and social community. As the period of the judges began its long decline, women became objects of men's foolish vows (Jephthah's daughter, 11:29–40), the objects of men's desire (14:1–3; 16:1), and the purchased instruments for schemes of male vengeance (16:5). This general decline from woman as the subject of independent action to woman as the object of men's actions and desires in the book of Judges coincides with the gradual decline in the health of Israel's social and religious life during the judges era. That decline culminates with the atrocity of rape and murder committed against the Levite's concubine in Judges 19:1, certainly one of the most brutal and violent scenes in all of Scripture. The interplay of an individual Israelite (Samson, Micah) or a particular tribe (Dan) functioning as a symbol or metaphor for all Israel is a narrative device that continues into Judges 19:1–21. Certainly the horror of the rape and murder of the Levite's concubine must be taken seriously in its own right as a matter of patriarchal violence against women. However, its juxtaposition with the fractious civil war in chaps. 20–21 invites the reader to consider the fate of this woman, who has been raped, murdered, and cut into twelve pieces, as a gruesome metaphor for the social body of the twelve-tribe union of Israel. Increasingly in the book of Judges, Israel has been dishonored, attacked, killed, and split into pieces by other Israelites. Hints of these internal tribal divisions and conflicts began already in the Song of Deborah and Barak in 5:15–17 and in Gideon's conflict with the Ephraimites and the people of

Penuel and Succoth (8:1–9, 13–17). The internal violence and social dissolution within Israel gradually escalated with Abimelech's murder of his seventy half-brothers (9:5), Jephthah's killing of 42,000 Ephraimites (12:1–6), Judah's betrayal of Samson to the Philistines (15:9–13), and Samson's unwillingness to lead any Israelite tribes in a coalition against the Philistines. The fabric of Israel's tribal union gradually unraveled into a disheveled heap of threads.[8]

The concubine in Judges 19 was a wife of secondary status, belonging (literally) to *a certain Levite* (19:1).[9] Levites were charged with serving and teaching Israel's law.[10] This included fostering the practice of hospitality.[11] The woman had left the Levite to return to her father's house.[12] The NRSV says, *Then her husband set out after her, to speak tenderly to her and bring her back* (19:3). The Hebrew text says that he went after her *to speak to her heart, to bring her back*.[13] The NJPS says, *to woo her and to win her back*.[14] We note

---

8. Olson, 872–3. Boling, *Judges*, 277: "It is impossible to do justice to this story without looking ahead to the last two chapters of the book, for the finale (chs. 20–21) represents the confederacy as utterly leaderless. The Israelites will overreact to one case of injustice in such a way as to compound the tragedy a thousand times over, and permit the situation to develop into a full–scale civil war. The reason has been given in the opening sentence of this chapter: Israel has been too busy ordering its affairs to have more than random regard for Yahweh."

9. Baab, 666, indicates that a concubine was a slave girl, acquired by purchase, taken as captive, or received as payment of debt; she would bear children to the master, might have certain rights, but was nevertheless the master's property. See Trible, 66.

10. Abba, 876–89; Deut 31:9–12.

11. Exod 22:21; 23:9; Lev 19:33–34; Deut 16:14; 26:12.

12. Olson, re: 19:2, notes that various translations enhance the reasons for which the woman had left. With no legal right to initiate a divorce, her leaving could be considered as adultery even though she had not necessarily committed adultery. The text may indicate the Levite's guilt more than that of the concubine. Myers, 809.

13. Trible, 67; Myers, 809.

14. Such language—*to bring her back, to speak to her heart, to woo and win her*— indicates love, restoration, and sympathy without specifying guilt (Gen 34:3; Hos 2:14). We could infer that he had been in the wrong, and she had

the man's initiative to overcome whatever reason for which she had left and to bring her home. Her exit is explained only by the statement that she *became angry with him, and she went away from him to her father's house* (NRSV 19:2).[15]

The Levite is greeted with lavish hospitality upon reception into the father–in–law's house.[16] He is dissuaded from leaving and the feasting and festivities continue for several days. The Levite finally departs with his concubine and animals. He has pressed onward to Gibeah in order to be among fellow Israelites (as over against foreigners, 19:12, at Jebus), no doubt expecting their friendship.

But friendship and provisions are not forthcoming from those of whom it had been anticipated. The travelers are finally received into the house of an old man (19:20). The old man's hospitality is "a glaring contrast to the coldness of the Benjaminites."[17] But then the situation takes a deadly turn, and hospitality runs to bizarre extremes as it goes horribly awry. We remember the Sodom episode in Genesis 19, as now the men of Gibeah surround the house, pound on the door, and demand that the male guest be brought outside, *so that we may have intercourse with him* (19:22).[18]

We note that the deflected *threat* posed by Sodom's men in Genesis 19 has been turned to violent *action* in Judges 19, as the men of Gibeah execute their evil intention.[19] Sodom was identified with the Canaanites, but Gibeah was inhabited by the

---

been the one wronged or abused, as does Boling, *Judges*, 274, "The Levite's concern to recover his concubine suggests that she, not he, is the offended party." See 273–4 for her anger.

15. Boling, "Judges," 401: "Israelite law did not allow for divorce by the wife. She became an adulteress by walking out." Some interpretations refer to her prostitution. Boling, *Judges*, 273, says, "But it is strange that the woman would become a prostitute and then run home."

16. Myers, 809, "Reconciliation would remove the disrepute brought on by separation. Feasting was in order."

17. Ibid., 812.

18. בְּנֵי־בְלִיַּעַל. (bənê-bəliyyáʿal ) are the "sons of Belial" (KJV), that is, sons of worthlessness or wickedness, of whom we read also in 1 Sam 2:12 and 1 Kings 21:10, 13; Myers, *Judges*, 812. NRSV calls them, "a perverse lot;" the NJPS says, "a depraved lot."

19. Is this the sin of Gibeah, of which the Prophet Hosea speaks (9:9; 10:9)?

Israelite tribe of Benjamin. It is thus not Canaanites, notorious for moral profligacy from Israelite perspective, but now *Israelites themselves* who have forsaken covenant righteousness in transgression of hospitality and Torah.

There are several similarities between the two stories in Genesis and Judges. One such is that the idea of homosexuality as the focus of the text is disabused by the fact that the men of Gibeah did in fact accept a female substitute in place of the male houseguest for whom they had clamored.[20] Her fate and the reaction to her death by the Levite increase the loathsome character of the story after the obligation to hospitality is acted out in grotesque and despicable ways. This is reminiscent of Lot's offered solution in Gen 19:8, except that here the gruesome story is allowed its horrific end.[21] Other similarities between the two texts include:

1. each of the cities is unfriendly toward visitors;

2. the travelers would have spent the night in the town square, except for a friendly man who showed hospitality;

3. in each case the friendly host is not native to the city;

4. aggressive men of the city surround the house;

5. the aggressors demand that the guest(s) come out to be used for sex;

6. the horrified host pleads with the crowd not to commit so evil a thing;

7. virgin daughters are offered as a substitute;

---

20. Hackett, "Women's Lives," 362, "The issue then does not seem to be one of sexual orientation (although it is often portrayed as such), since the men were eventually willing to settle for raping a female."

21. Scanzoni and Mollenkott, 57: "This story of rape and murder is hardly rendered any more palatable by the fact that the host offered his daughter to spare the guest, and the guest presented his own wife to spare himself. In the ancient Middle East, writes Roman Catholic scholar John McKenzie, 'that the woman should be sacrificed to spare the man was simply taken for granted.'" See McKenzie, *The World of the Judges*, 165. On the depicted threat to manly honor see Nissinen, 50–51.

8. the hostility of the city and the hospitality of the man are juxtaposed;

9. each story is preceded by an account of special hospitality: Abraham in Gen 18:1–5, and the father of the Levite's wife in Jud 19:3–10.[22]

Although the congruence of the stories in Genesis 19 and Judges 19 is quite striking, the Judges 19 episode has its own peculiarities. We note:

1. in Sodom the guests were angels; in Gibeah they were ordinary human beings, thus accounting for the different outcomes;

2. in Gibeah the host offers the aggressors one of his guests, the concubine;

3. the aggressors were satisfied after receiving the concubine and they did not insist on having the Levite or the virgin daughter;

4. once the victim of rape fell at the threshold of the house no one inside seemed to hear or check on her, as though they were asleep;

5. the brutality of the attack is repeatedly emphasized (*all night, until morning, when dawn broke*) but not only was she not checked on but the Levite prepared to depart as though nothing had happened, and upon seeing the concubine's body he tells her to get up and make ready to leave;

6. the cutting and sending of the body is a perpetuation of violence and may be taken as a sign or warning of what will now transpire against enemies or those who refused to join the pursuit and punishment of the aggressors.[23]

The text is not explicit about whether the woman was already dead when her master found her at the threshold in the morning.

22. Nissinen, 50.

23. Amit, 552. Such action seems to have been the purpose of Saul's butchering of oxen for use as a warning of retaliation against his enemies (1 Sam 11:7).

We might infer that she was alive, or that he thought she was alive, as he spoke to her as expecting a response. Would it not seem strange to speak in such an abrupt, or even gruff manner as when he commanded that she get up and make ready to depart? It is a strange way to treat a person who has been abused all night long. "Where are the words that speak to her heart? Certainly not here."[24] He had set out *to speak tenderly to her and bring her back* (19:3), to speak to her heart. But the intention is nowhere translated into fact. The facts of the story are these:

1. the concubine had left because she was angry at the master; we could infer it was something he had done to her that was the cause of the original trouble;

2. he had set out to win her back and bring her home, thus suggesting that it was his responsibility to right a wrong and initiate the restoration;

3. when trouble occurred it was he who had seized her (indicating rough or gruff handling) and forced her outside the house;

4. during her night of abuse, rape, and torture he had gone to bed and slept;

5. in the morning he made ready to leave, and only when ready did he open the door and go out of the house;

6. upon finding her lying at the threshold he took no action to pick her up, give her aid, or even speak tenderly to her; it would not be inconsistent with these actions (and inactions) that his was also the hand that ended her life.[25]

A civil war ensues, with Israel arrayed in punishment against the tribe of Benjamin. The bloody conflict brings harm to Israel as a whole, *because the LORD had made a breach in the tribes of Israel*

24. Trible, 79. Trible points out that the Greek (LXX) text says that the woman is dead, while the Hebrew text is silent on the matter, allowing for the possibility that she is yet alive.

25. Olson, 876; Hackett, "Women's Lives," 361.

(21:15).[26] The book ends with the repeated theme of lawlessness and disappointment in the judges: *In those days there was no king in Israel; all the people did what was right in their own eyes* (21:25).

## Summary

If the purpose of such a story and set of scenes as Judges 19–21 were to serve and illustrate beyond all doubt the consequence of its major theme, that in those days there was no king, no adherence to law, no civil authority, and hence no civility, then the scenes constitute a ringing success. This, indeed, must be taken as the purpose and function of the book itself. The episodes involving the concubine and men of Gibeah, the collapse of Israel into civil war, the near eradication of one of the tribes, and the need for a king serve such purpose and function. It would be violence to the text of Scripture to pull from its fabric one single thread, in this case 19:22, and apply to life in our present time a presumed meaning for that single thread.

The point of the Genesis 19 Sodom account, followed by the Gibeah episode in Judges 19, is the absence of righteousness resulting in the breakdown of civil society and covenant community. The violent evil of gang rape and the desire to prove conquest and power over strangers signals the failure of hospitality and the pervasiveness of general lawlessness. Chaos, violence, and abuse follow. In fact, none of the further references to Sodom in the Bible mention homosexual acts, but concentrate instead on such sins as greed, injustice, inhospitality, excess wealth, indifference to the poor, and general wickedness.[27]

---

26. Amit, 557, "The blow struck to the Benjaminites harmed the overall structure of the Israelite tribes."

27. Rogers, 71. We note that in Judges 19 the sins of Sodom have invaded a tribe of Israel. The scale of this invasion of sin is carried by a common pattern in Judges: the people did what was evil in the sight of the Lord (3:7); the anger of the Lord was kindled against Israel and he sold them into dominance by foreign powers; the Israelites cried out for help; the Lord sent a deliverer (3:9) who delivered them. The cycle repeats itself. See Boling, "Judges," 367–369, who indicates that the noun *judge* occurs only once after 2:16–19, while the reference to *deliverer/savior* is prevalent.

The sin of the men of Sodom relates essentially to violence, abuse, rape, humiliation, and subjugation of other persons, particularly strangers, outsiders, and the similarly vulnerable. It is the *others, the different,* who are so easily perceived as threat. The stories caution us against unchecked attitudes and actions against those who *are* different from us. They describe the need for the civil use and authority of law, both within the community of faith and the society at large.

The Sodom and Gibeah stories are not about homosexuality. They speak of breakdown in the very structure of civilized society, the neglect of covenant among those who are chosen and called, the resulting destruction that lands not always on the perpetrators but often on the innocent, and the carnage that ensues when individualism and anarchy rule the day in place of authentic and just government. The stories of Genesis 19 and Judges 19 graphically depict the need for the covenant people to find a righteous way to live in community, and thus serve and enable a society that is civil, just, and humane.

The same can be said for the church of our own time. One could see here an example of the need for the church to *model for its world* the new creation in Christ, love as the law of Christ, and how to be the concomitant new humanity. So to model could be perceived as the church's mission. As we turn to Leviticus we may wonder whether the same issues are therein addressed as in Genesis and Judges. We may wonder also whether the statutes of Leviticus provide the better way for which we seek, the need for which has been so clearly identified by these stories of cruelty and abuse.

# 5

## Freedom's Fence

*Leviticus 18:1–30*

### PROHIBITION AND PUNISHMENT

LEVITICUS HAS AN INDEPENDENT identity among the five Books
of the Law.[1] Its theme and content follow its Hebrew name, *Torat
Kohanim*, the Priests' Manual. And yet the laws of this manual are
not for priests alone and its teachings do not relate solely to worship and ritual. In Leviticus, ethics inform the rituals and the ritual
actions issue in a moral basis for life itself. The Book of Exodus
that *precedes* Leviticus describes the construction of the sacred

1. Anderson, 3, 11: "Today the Jewish people refer to their scriptures
as *Tanak*, an acronym made up of the initial consonants of the three major
divisions of the Hebrew Bible: Torah ('Law'), Nebi'im ('Prophets'), and Kethu-
bim ('Writings') . . . the section of the Hebrew Bible that is regarded as most
authoritative by Jewish tradition (includes) the books of Genesis, Exodus,
Leviticus, Numbers, and Deuteronomy. The Hebrew word for these five books
is *Torah*, often translated inadequately as 'Law', but better rendered as 'Teaching'. . . . Scholars also refer to these books as the Pentateuch . . .'the book of the
five scrolls.'"

religious objects used in Israel's rituals including the tabernacle, its contents, and the priestly vestments. The Book of Numbers that *follows* Leviticus concentrates on laws of the Israelite camp as it is in motion on its exodus journey from oppression in Egypt to freedom in the Promised Land.[2]

But Leviticus itself is about the everyday lives of people in the covenant community. It is filled with "scenes from the living cult."[3] Leviticus law applies to persons, relationships in community, and corporate identity as over against that of Israel's neighbors. It shows the order, boundaries, and expectation of God's covenant with Israel in great detail. Thus, "The Levitical laws mean to regulate the common life in Israel, paying particular attention to issues of sexuality which are of special importance to tribes, clans, or extended families living in close physical proximity. At stake is the protection of the community and its social structures, a concern which apparently takes precedence, at least in the matters listed here, over the free expression of the individual."[4]

The texts about *same gender sexual acts or practices* are within the Holiness Code of Leviticus 17–26.[5] Two verses in chapters 18 and 20 comprise Israel's early legislation against same gender sexual practices, along with prohibitions against eating meat with the blood, wearing garments made of two kinds of yarn, planting fields with two kinds of seed, and the wearing of tattoos.[6] Leviticus

2. Milgrom, "Leviticus," 151–3.

3. Ibid., 151; Schwartz, "Leviticus," 203–6.

4. Gaiser, "Homosexuality," 164.

5. *Same gender sexual acts or practices* is appropriate terminology for reference to the texts under consideration, rather than treating the texts as referring to homosexuality, the word by which we can indicate a personal orientation to life or a condition of one's person. That is, *homosexuality* will hereafter refer to one's *being*, as distinct from a person's *actions* or practices. The biblical texts under consideration seem to refer to the latter, but not the former.

6. Scanzoni and Mollenkott, 60. Leviticus 17–26 is distinct in content and theme from chapters 1–16. These two sources of content are often abbreviated as P for Priestly (1–16) and H for Holiness (17–26). Within Leviticus itself we find a contrast between two aspects of holiness. In the Priestly Code of chapters 1–16 there is a spatial holiness that attends the sanctuary. This part of Leviticus focuses on the priesthood and its work of teaching the distinction

17–26 extends holiness beyond the sanctuary and priesthood to the Promised Land and thence to all the people of Israel. The emphasis on land and people in the land is critical for the study of these texts. This extension follows logically from the concept of spatial holiness: because the land is holy all its residents are to keep the land holy.[7]

The two Torah texts that speak of same gender sexual actions in Leviticus 18 and 20 do so in ways different from Genesis and Judges. The Leviticus texts that refer to same gender sexual activity indicate *prohibition* on the one hand and *punishment* on the other. These instructions intend to help demarcate Israel from its neighbors and predecessors in the land.

## LEVITICUS 18:22 (1–30)

Leviticus 18 regulates sexual relations. The concern is that Israel *not* be like the peoples of Egypt, the land they have exited, nor like Canaan, the land to which they are being brought. Israel shall *not* follow those peoples' practices: "You shall not copy the practices of the land of Egypt where you dwelt, or of the land of Canaan to which I am taking you; nor shall you follow their laws" (18:3 NJPS).

Sexual relations are prohibited with kin (6–18), with a menstruating woman (19), or with a kinsman's wife (20). Child sacrifice is forbidden (21). Sexual relations between men are forbidden (22). Sex with animals is forbidden (23). Israel is to learn from other nations' experience and apply such lessons to itself: "Do not

---

between what is holy and what is common and between what is clean or unclean (10:10). Israel's moral sins and physical impurities bring pollution of the sanctuary and with it will come expulsion from the land. Therefore, the priests must teach Israel not to defile themselves and also purge the sanctuary when it becomes defiled. Holiness of persons is limited to priests and Nazirites in Leviticus 1–16 and is constricted to the sanctuary and its priests. Pollution of the sanctuary is due to Israel's moral and ritual violations committed anywhere in the camp. These need to be removed by purification offering, sacrifice, and confession (16:3–22).

7. D. Wright, "Leviticus," 169: "In contrast to the earlier Priestly Torah treatment of sacrifices at the beginning of Leviticus, the focus here, in the Holiness Collection, is on the lay Israelite."

defile yourselves in any of these ways, for by all these practices the nations I am casting out before you have defiled themselves. Thus the land became defiled; and I punished it for its iniquity, and the land vomited out its inhabitants. But you shall keep my statutes and my ordinances . . . otherwise the land will vomit you out for defiling it . . . I am the LORD your God" (Lev 18:24–25, 26, 28, 30).

We note two specific aspects of the injunctions. First, the prohibitions protect the people from defiling and therefore losing the *land*. If the prohibitions are transgressed, the land will vomit out the Israelites, as the former inhabitants had been vomited out.[8] Second, the prohibitions protect the people from the loss or destruction of *progeny*. In this sense the theme is procreation. The emission of semen that is lost, or that happens during incest and thus issues in illicit progeny, or the destruction of progeny by sacrifice to Molech, are the practices to be shunned.[9] This could explain why the Hebrew Scriptures contain no prohibition against female same sex relations: no emission of semen is involved.[10]

The English text of Leviticus 18:22 reads, "You shall not lie with a male as with a woman; it is an abomination."[11] In this rendering of v. 22 the two key nouns are in the singular, *man* and *woman*. The effect of the translation is to make the sense of the verse generic and

8. For the significance of the land in the biblical narrative, see Brueggemann, *Land*, xv, where he explains, "The study is organized around three histories of the land: (a) the history of promise into the *land*, (b) the history of management into *exile*, and (c) the new history of promise which begins in exile and culminates in *kingdom* . . . The recital of the three histories is not a neat scheme, but a slow torturous process."

9. This is analogous to the story of Onan, Gen 38:9–10, who deliberately spilled semen on the ground during coitus so as to avoid impregnating his brother's wife. For more on the importance of semen in the narrative of holiness see Knust, ch. 6, and for the Onan episode, 216–17.

10. Schwartz, "Leviticus," 251. See Knust, 146–7.

11. The Hebrew word תּוֹעֵבָה (*to'eba*), indicates what is ritually or ethically loathsome or repugnant. It can include prohibited foods, violation of custom, imperfect sacrifices, sexual irregularities, moral or ethical faults, reversal of the natural, and idolatrous practices. See Lovelace, 12–13. The LXX and NT translate this word with the Greek βδέλυγμα (*bdelugma*), as in Matt 24:15 and Mark 13:14 (desolating sacrilege), Luke 16:15 and Rev 17:4-5; 21:27 (abomination). See Toombs, 641–8.

all-inclusive. That is, a man shall not lie with any other man as he would (lie) with a woman. Is this the truest or only sense of the text?

## JACOB MILGROM

Milgrom represents the first of three lines of interpretation that will be briefly summarized.[12] Milgrom draws attention to a strange feature of Lev 18:22. The verb, *lie*, together with the phrases, *with a male* and *with a woman* is a conflation of ideas that go unnoticed in the English text. The verse literally reads, "You shall not lie with a male as the lyings down of a woman."[13] Why the plural, *lyings down*? The answer to which Milgrom points is in the context and text itself. The context enumerates specific females with whom a man's sexual intercourse is forbidden. The common phrase, *to uncover nakedness*, is a euphemism for sexual intercourse.[14] The forbidden sexual relations include:

- your mother, your father's wife, 7–8;
- your sister, your father's/mother's daughter, 9;
- your son's daughter, your daughter's daughter, 10;
- your father's wife's daughter begotten by your father, 11;
- your father's sister, 12;
- your mother's sister, 13;
- your father's brother's wife, 14;
- your daughter-in-law, 15;
- your brother's wife, 16;

12. Jacob Milgrom (1923–2010) wrote the three-volume commentary on Leviticus in the *Anchor Bible Commentary*. His work is considered the gold standard on the book of Leviticus. He spent his scholarly career studying, teaching, and writing about the Torah, and specialized in the study of purity laws. He was a professor emeritus at the U. of California.

13. Milgrom, *Leviticus 17–22*, 1569. Knust, 147–148, points out that there are no other such laws in the Hebrew Bible. The two references in Leviticus, "are therefore entirely exceptional."

14. D. Wright, "Leviticus," 168fn. v. 6.

- a woman and daughter, her son's daughter, her daughter's daughter, 17;

- a woman as rival to her sister, 18;

- a woman in her menstrual uncleanness, 19;

- a kinsman's wife, 20.

These sexual relations for a man are forbidden with any of the specifically listed women within his own extended family. The list is then followed by v. 22 and its extended prohibition, *You shall not lie with a male as the lyings down with a woman* . . . But rather than referring to any or all male–male sexual relations, Milgrom sees v. 22 logically relating to the preceding list of forbidden relationships with women in vv. 7–20. The relations with women that are forbidden to a man are likewise forbidden to a man with men to whom he is similarly related.[15]

The prohibition is about these specific illicit sexual relations within the family.[16] Therefore, sexual relations are forbidden between a man and father, brother, son, grandson, nephew, stepson, and so on. As certain *lyings with a woman* are forbidden, so also certain *lyings with a man* are accordingly forbidden. Same sex intercourse, ". . . is herewith forbidden for only the equivalent degree of forbidden heterosexual relations, namely those enumerated in the preceding verses."[17]

---

15. The Hebrew, מִשְׁכְּבֵי אִשָּׁה (*mišKebê 'iššâ*) is a technical term that in the plural refers to illicit carnal relations, *lyings down with a woman,* indicating forbidden relations with women who are within the man's extended family.

16. See also Gen 49:4, like Lev 18:22 and 20:13.

17. Milgrom, *Leviticus*, 1569, says, "And since the same term *miškebê 'iššāh* is used in the list containing sanctions (20:13), it would mean that sexual liaisons with males, falling outside the control of the paterfamilias, would be neither condemnable nor punishable. Thus *miškebê 'iššāh* referring to illicit male–female relations, is applied to illicit male–male relations . . . In effect, this means that the homosexual prohibition applies to Ego with father, son, and brother . . . and to grandfather–grandson, uncle–nephew, and stepfather–stepson, but not to any other male." He wrote similarly in *Bible Review* (December, 1993).

The forbidden relations apply to Israelite men within the land and within the family. Sexual relations are forbidden for the male with females within the extended family and sexual relations with males within the family are also prohibited. Other males (not Israelite, not in the land, not within the family) are not included in these prohibitions. The Israelite male of the normal, non-familial, male–female sexual relationship is here addressed and instructed not to play the same male part in relation to another familial man. Such male–male sex would be an abomination.[18]

Legal regulations surround the relationship of Israel and its Lord, guarding against idolatry, breakdown of covenant, and loss of land. Separation from other allegiances, nations, and practices is intrinsic to covenant and Israel's holiness. Holiness is served by laws regarding ceremonial cleanness and uncleanness. Leviticus 19 enhances the teaching about holiness with instructions that include reverence for parents and Sabbath keeping (v. 3), shunning idols and images (v. 4), acceptable sacrifices (vv. 4–8), instructions for reaping and gleaning the harvest, and leaving some in the fields for the poor (vv. 9–10). There are laws against stealing, false dealing, lying, swearing falsely by God's name, profaning God's name, defrauding the neighbor, and abuse of the poor, the deaf, the blind, and the laborer (vv. 11–16). Leviticus 19:17–18 instructs against hate, vengeance, slander, and bearing a grudge. In sharp contrast to the sins and profanations listed in Leviticus 19, the text

---

18. Knust, 148–9, ". . . the interdicition in Leviticus is addressed specifically to the insertive partner in the sex act, not the receptive partner. It is the penetrator who is instructed not to engage in the 'lying down of the woman' with a man . . . The problem with 'lying with a man as with a woman,' then, is that it involves the confusion of appropriate gender roles . . . while also spilling semen in a situation where pregnancy cannot take place." See Boyarin, 343: "When one man 'uses' another man as a female, he causes a transgression of the borders between male and female." Knust, 149, "The mixing that Leviticus seeks to avoid . . . is the act of gender-bending, in which the receptive partner is assimilated to the category of 'woman' by being anally penetrated . . . The sole target of this commandment is an Israelite man who anally penetrates another Israelite man . . ."

continues (v. 18) with an instruction that will resound throughout Scripture . . . *you shall love your neighbor as yourself.*[19]

## MARY DOUGLAS

Douglas offers three keys to help unlock the message of Leviticus.[20] One key is her analysis of the *structure* of Leviticus 18–20 and how the structure highlights the focus of the message and teaching of this part of the book. Another key is examination of laws that function as *analogies*. Such laws are affected because they are like other laws. A third key is recognition of the difference between a person's basic sexual *orientation* in life, the way one is, as over against sexual *actions and practices*, what one does.

First, with respect to structure, Douglas notes that the relationship of texts to one another in context is instructive about the main message. The prohibitions and punishments of chapters 18 and 20 function in such a way as to highlight the central theme of God's righteousness or justice in chapter 19.[21] The three chapters form a trilogy in which 18 and 20 are the frame around the central thought in 19. The place of priority or honor in the middle of the trilogy is held by the emphasis in chapter 19 on the righteousness or justice

---

19. See Matt 22:37–40, Mark 12:28–33, Luke 10:27, Rom 13:9, Gal 5:14, and Jesus' teaching about love for God and the neighbor, on which hangs *all the law and the prophets, there is no other commandment greater than these.* Paul affirms, *Love is the fulfilling of the law . . . the whole law is summed up in (this) single commandment.*

20. Mary Douglas (1921–2007) was a British anthropologist who taught at University College of London, the Russell Sage Institute of New York, and Northwestern University. Her special interests were in human culture, symbolism, the study of purity and taboos, and comparative religions. Her reputation as a careful and pioneering scholar was established by her book, *Purity and Danger* (1966). This work argued that the kosher laws were neither primitive health regulations nor religious tests of faith. The kosher laws rather functioned to establish boundary maintenance (for the sake of the faith community's identity definition), forbidding foods that did not fall into a specific category. Her work on Leviticus is held in high regard.

21. Douglas, "Justice," 341–350.

of God. The righteous judgments and ordinances of the LORD are in sharp contrast to the gods and practices of Egypt and Canaan.[22]

Leviticus 18:1–5 accomplishes emphasis by repetition. Twice we find, *my ordinances, my statutes,* and three times, *I am the LORD (your God).* There are warnings against the idolatry of being like those other gods, other peoples, and their practices. The ethical standards of God's righteousness reach their culmination in the summary of covenant law: *You shall love your neighbor as yourself* (19:18), a standard that extends even to the treatment of aliens in the land: *You shall love the alien as yourself* (19:34). The *pedimental composition* of the three chapters first slopes up to the high point, the climax or apex of the passage, and then slopes back down again.[23] Chapter 18, the upward slope, prepares for what we find in chapter 19. Chapter 20 shows the consequences of chapter 19. What Douglas calls the *hair-raising anathemas* of chapters 18 and 20, the assertive prohibitions and strident punishments, receive their real impact from chapter 19.[24]

22. Douglas, *Leviticus as Literature*, 240, emphasizes the cultic nature of these texts in relation to worshipping communities. The practices of neighboring cults are abominations from which Israel shall distinguish and separate itself lest the land be defiled and lost (18:26–30). The "delayed completion" of ch. 19 comes in its counterpart in 26.

23. A pediment is the triangular construction over the cornice or portico of a building. One can also think of a pyramid, the side angles of which draw attention to the apex.

24. Douglas, "Justice," 342; *Leviticus*, 236: "There could not be a stronger framing of the central chapter at the apex of the pediment. Leviticus' scheme very deliberately puts the laws of righteous and honest dealings at the center and the sexual sins at the periphery . . . The laws on each side against incest, sodomy, and bestiality are backed by twice-repeated warnings that the land will vomit the people out if they follow these cults. The anathemas are not laws about everyday affairs. If they were intended to provide guidance for the organization of marriage, the choice of marriage partners, or about wrong and right conduct of family life and sex, they would have to be judged strangely inadequate. They say nothing about inheritance, divorce, or succession. The context is inescapably cultic. The perorations refer to defilement of the land, a grave situation which results from idolatry . . . These laws are about defilement by idolatry."

The effect of using these unedifying sexual deviations framing chapter 19 is to feature the concepts of righteousness, liberty, and justice, which it expounds in the middle. These chapters contrast the pure and noble character of the Hebrew God with the libidinous customs of the very strange false gods.[25]

We note the two corresponding statements at Lev 19:2 and 19:37: *You shall be holy, for I the LORD your God am holy*, and, *You shall keep . . . all my ordinances and observe them: I am the LORD.* The holiness of God is the cause, the effect of which is the people's holiness. We then note specific characteristics of this holiness: frequent echoes of the Ten Commandments (3, 4, 11, 12, 13); concern for the poor (9–10), the laborer (13), the aged (32), the alien (33); concern for the deaf and the blind (14); injunctions against fraud (13), partiality of judgment (15), and vengeance and grudge (18); great concern for the land (23, 29); care for integrity of weights and measures (36); reiteration of certain sexual regulations (20–22, 29).

Just as the righteousness of God generates the ethics of the people, so the ethical reminders are anchored in exodus deliverance (19:36) and in the repeated reminders of the divine name. The name, *YHWH*, was given for Moses to relay to the people, and for the people to call on throughout all generations.[26]

The laws on either side of this apex of teaching, the laws against sexual sins, are thereby placed deliberately at the periphery in deference to the teaching's true center: God's righteousness.[27] This focus in the middle of the three chapters has at *its* center the rule of love (19:18): "The rule that astonishes Christians who did

---

25. Douglas, *Leviticus*, 237, maintains that the cults of Egypt and Canaan practiced prostitution in their temples, there was incest by the Pharaohs, worship rites included sexual connections with animals, and the use of menstrual blood was part of pacts made with demons.

26. The name (Exodus 3) in Hebrew, יְהֹוָה (YHWH, probably pronounced *Yahweh* with the supplying of vowels), is translated as κύριος (*Kyrios*) in the Greek text of the Septuagint (LXX), and is represented by the word LORD in full caps in the English text of such Bible translations as NRSV. See Fretheim, *Exodus*, 62–67, for how "*The name shapes Israel's story, and the story gives greater texture to the name.*" (63–64).

27. Douglas, "Justice," 345.

not remember that it came from the Old Testament is revealed as the cornerstone of holiness teaching."[28]

The second key that Douglas offers relates to analogies. The prohibitions against same gender sexual practices may have been in effect partly because they were like other laws. They may be examples of law that make sense by analogy. So Douglas explains:

> Leviticus' literary style is correlative, it works through analogies. Instead of explaining why an instruction has been given, or even what it means, it adds another similar instruction, and another and another, thus producing its highly schematized effect. The series of analogies locate a particular instance in a context. They expand the meaning. Sometimes the analogies are hierarchized, one within another making inclusive sets, or sometimes they stand in opposed pairs or contrast sets. They serve in place of causal explanations. If one asks, "Why this rule?" the answer is that it conforms to that other rule . . . In Leviticus the patterning of oppositions and inclusions is generally all the explaining that we are going to get. Instead of argument there is analogy.[29]

This pattern holds true also with respect to the punishment prescribed in 20:13. Just as chapter 18 names the prohibitions, so chapter 20 names the punishments. The punishments in ch. 20 are grouped according to the penalty that is meted out, just as the prohibitions in chapter 18 are grouped according to what they protect. Thus in ch. 18, "Thou shalt not lie with a man as one lies with a woman, is in parallel with the prohibition against adultery with a neighbour's wife, both are intended to protect the married state."[30] Similarly, in ch. 20, ". . . homosexual acts are set at the same level of gravity as adultery. A community which is determined to live by the law would take them equally seriously, and no one who would

28. Ibid., 349.

29. Douglas, *Leviticus*, 18. The key is comparison and consistency: *this* is like *that* so both are true.

30. Ibid., 239.

tolerate an adulterer in the community would be able consistently to persecute a homosexual."[31]

The third key provided by Douglas is the distinction between sexual orientation and sexual actions. What is spoken of both in terms of the sexual prohibition in Lev 18:22 and the punishment in 20:13 is not what a person *is* but what a person *does*. Thus, not orientation but action is the target of legislation. Douglas suggests that the idea of orientation was simply not in the thinking of the time, and what the laws legislate against are the homosexual actions of heterosexual persons: ". . . the idea of homosexuality as a condition of a person was not envisaged: what Leviticus forbids is not homosexuality as understood today (in other words, a permanent orientation), but homosexual acts performed by heterosexuals (for example, the molestation described in Genesis 19:4–5)."[32]

We note that Lev 19:19 prohibits allowing two kinds of animals to breed together, two kinds of seed to be sown in the same field, and two kinds of material to be made into the same garment. This is an echo of what Douglas calls *uneven complementarity*. It includes the uneven fate or outcomes of two goats, one set free as the scapegoat, one sacrificed (16:9); two birds, one set free, one sacrificed for a leper's cleansing (14:6–7); two brothers, Isaac and Ishmael (Genesis 16); two other brothers, Jacob and Esau (Genesis 28–35); two kingdoms, Northern–Israel (Samaria), and Southern–Judah (Jerusalem).[33]

Furthermore, "There is an echo of the injunction in Leviticus 19:19 not to join grossly uneven pairs, whether cattle, seed, or textiles: 'You shall not let your cattle breed with a different kind; you shall not sow your field with two kinds of seed; nor

---

31. Ibid., 239.

32. Ibid., 238 (citing Maccoby, "Abomination," 17).

33. Ibid., 250. Milgrom, "Leviticus," 182: "God separated everything according to its species (Genesis 1). The human world should mirror the natural world. Israel, therefore, may not mix with other nations, but be holy, set apart for God."

shall there come upon you a garment of cloth made of two kinds of stuff.' (Lev 19:19)."[34]

And yet there is often no moral causation or condemnation connected to the uneven or differently fated side of the division:

> There is no judgment against Ishmael, he is neither immoral nor destined to an unhappy or godless life. He is not condemned, he is free to roam the wilderness and will be a great prince. He is like the bird and the goat which were not chosen, while Isaac is parallel to the goat or the bird on which the lot of the Lord fell, destined to a sacred calling . . . God's choice is unconstrained . . . election is never deserved. The converse is also true: demerit does not explain misfortune; disease or barrenness is not the fault of the victim.[35]

This line of thought could be a way to understand the nature of things as they are, that is, the *natural or like-to-like*. Just as the mixing of uneven pairs is warned against in 19:19, so also Leviticus warns against the mixing or *uneven complementarity* of same gender union.

The theme of God's righteousness reflects the central teaching of Leviticus as a whole.[36] The theme will reverberate throughout Scripture and come to find its privileged place in the teaching of Jesus and the missionary message of Paul. Above the ethical and ritual commands "soars the commandment to love all persons (19:18), including aliens (19:34). Such love must be concretely expressed in deeds . . ."[37] Here love prevails over law. Indeed, love *is* law![38]

---

34. Douglas, *Leviticus*, 250.

35. Ibid., 251.

36. Ibid., 5, 235–238.

37. Milgrom, "Leviticus," 182.

38. Wills, *What Jesus Meant*, 32–39, discusses, "Are Some Still Unclean?" At stake in our ethical struggles is the question of the character of God. Gaiser, "Preaching," 209, concludes, "Love is who the God of the Bible is."

## ROBERT GAGNON

Gagnon emphasizes the created order and the divinely established categories of that order in his understanding of the Leviticus sexuality texts.[39] Two concerns are at the heart of Gagnon's view: (1) the divinely instituted created order itself, and, (2) human responsibility for gender complementarity within that order.

Concern for the created order is reflected in Gagnon's referencing the categories of creation. Holiness means keeping the categories distinct.[40] Thus, "All the laws in Lev 18:6–23; 20:2–21 legislate against forms of sexual behavior that disrupt the created order set into motion by the God of Israel. Each of the laws has as its intent the channeling of male sexual impulses into a particular pattern of behavior, a pattern conducive to the healthy functioning of a people set apart to serve God's holy purposes."[41]

Same gender sexual intercourse mixes categories, confuses gender and bodily function, and is a conscious denial of God's design: ". . . God created distinct sexes, designed them for sexual pairing, and did so for a reason."[42] Concern for human responsibility is reflected in the way Gagnon speaks of "the very creatures whom God placed in charge of the good, ordered creation." That charge includes refraining from *gender bending* of human sexuality and care for the holistic complementarity or *fittedness* of male and female anatomy, physiology, and procreative powers. Complementarity is absent in male-to-male sexual activity and this problem has priority over degradation of status and failure to procreate in the laws of Leviticus.[43] We note three other aspects of Gagnon's view. First, he translates Lev 18:22 as singular: "With a male you

39. Robert Gagnon (b. 1958) is Assistant Professor of New Testament at Pittsburgh Theological Seminary. His scholarly study of same-sex erotic behavior is entitled, *The Bible and Homosexual Practice.*

40. Gagnon, *Practice*, 135 n. 212 (quoting Douglas, *Danger*, 53: ". . . holiness requires that different classes of things shall not be confused . . . Holiness means keeping distinct the categories of creation").

41. Ibid., 136.

42. Ibid., 142.

43. Ibid., 138–139.

shall not lie as though lying with a woman; it is an abomination."[44] Second, he understands the laws of 18:22 and 20:13 as, "unqualified and absolute. They neither penalize only oppressive forms of homosexuality nor excuse either party to the act."[45] Third, he sees the absolute prohibitions of Leviticus carried over into the New Testament: "The position adopted by Paul in the New Testament is not an aberration but is consistent with the heritage present in his Scriptures. The two covenants are in agreement."[46]

The second document by Gagnon to which we refer is a direct and detailed response to Milgrom's commentary on Leviticus. His critique makes three main points in response to Milgrom's views on Lev 18:22 and 20:13. Gagnon argues that the Leviticus texts, (1) are not simply laws about the lack of progeny or the wasting of seed, (2) are not only about incestuous homosexual unions, and (3) are not morally irrelevant for Gentiles not living in Israel.[47]

Regarding the problem of progeny, Gagnon maintains that Milgrom's view is a "fixation on the issue of procreation . . ." and that the larger issue is the problem of mixing of categories or discordant mergers. For a man to lie with a man as though lying with a woman is a "category error, a merger of two beings that are incongruous in terms of anatomy, procreative potential, and an array of personality features."[48]

Regarding the problem of incestuous unions, Gagnon maintains that the plural in Lev 18:22 (*lyings down*) is neutral rather than illicit. Other uses of the term in the Pentateuch, whether singular or plural, point to a neutrality and the argument about the illicit nature of the term is not convincing.[49]

Regarding the problem of the moral relevance of the Leviticus texts for Gentiles, Gagnon says that the ban on male–male intercourse has little to do with venue. The ban is not limited to

44. Ibid., 111.
45. Ibid., 115.
46. Ibid., 117.
47. Gagnon, "Critique," 2–9, 10–13, 13–17.
48. Ibid., 3, 4.
49. Ibid., 9–10, pointing to Num 31:17–18; Judg 21:11–12; Gen 49:4.

the land of Israel. Gagnon continues, "That is to say, such inter-course was not regarded by the authors of the Holiness Code as an 'abomination,' 'an abhorrent thing,' or 'something detestable, loathsome, utterly repugnant, disgusting' because it was commit-ted in the land of Israel but foremost because it ran counter to God's own design in creation."[50]

Gagnon, like Milgrom and Douglas, offers much to consider in our reading of Leviticus. We should, however, reflect on three aspects of Gagnon's study. One consideration relates to his view of the concept of categories. Is the concept of *categories of creation* as *the privileged interpretive device* appropriate for dealing with Torah texts generally and with Lev 18:22 and 20:13 in particular? We could note, by way of contrast, the prominence of the concept of *land* in God's covenant with Israel in texts such as these: "Go . . . to the land that I will show you" (Gen 12:1); "I have come down to deliver them . . . to bring them up out of that land to a good and broad land . . ." (Ex 3:8); "But you shall keep my statutes and my ordinances and commit none of these abominations . . . otherwise the land will vomit you out for defiling it . . ." (Lev 18:26–28). Thus, with respect to land as a dominant theme in Israel's story, Brueggemann says:

> Land is a central, if not *the central theme* of biblical faith.
> Biblical faith is a pursuit of historical belonging that in-cludes a sense of destiny derived from such belonging
> . . . land might be a way of organizing biblical theology
> . . . a fresh look at the Bible suggests that a sense of place
> is a primary category of faith . . . a yearning for a place is
> a decision to enter history with an identifiable people in
> an identifiable pilgrimage . . . The land for which Israel
> yearns and which it remembers is never unclaimed space
> but is always *a place with Yahweh*, a place well filled with
> memories of life with him and promise from him and
> vows to him. It is land that provides the central assurance
> to Israel of its historicality, that it will be and always must

50. Ibid., 14.

be concerned with actual rootage in a place which is a repository for commitment and therefore identity.[51]

Land is intimately connected to God's promise of deliverance *from* oppression in the land of Egypt and deliverance *to* a good land of Israel's own. And yet, land has no prominence in the creation narratives.

A second reflection revisits 18:22 and the plural, *lyings down*. Is the interpretation of the phrase as it relates to extended family contradicted by other texts where the words (either singular or plural) mean something else? This question involves the context of 18:22.

We note how 18:22 is introduced by v. 6 and summarized by v. 24: "None of you shall approach anyone near of kin to uncover nakedness," and, "Do not defile yourselves in any of these ways . . ." The inclusiveness of *anyone near of kin* and *any of these ways* is circumscribed by the list of relations that are prohibited. There is continuity between the *lyings down* in v. 22 and the prohibitions in vv. 6–23 and referenced in v. 24. It makes sense to see the prohibition of v. 22 in the light of kinship. There is a markedly high level of concern for the land: do not do as they do in the lands of Egypt and Canaan in the land to which I am bringing you (v. 3), lest you defile the land and it vomits you out (v. 25). It is credible to read the chapter in light of extended family relations within the land.

A third consideration issues in a question. Should categories of creation be imposed on our understanding of the New Testament? To put this question in another way, can certain dynamics of the old covenant serve as the interpretive center from which the new covenant is believed and understood? The new covenant is anchored in the Messiah, crucified and raised. Paul understood himself to be a minister of this new covenant that is of the Spirit, not of letter, life–giving, not death–bringing, and characterized by justification, not by condemnation.[52]

We will thus be prompted to the new covenant's own proclamation, including the parts wherein Paul presents his gospel, and

51. Brueggemann, *Land*, 3–7; Anderson, 110–50.

52. See Matt 26:28 and parallels; Rom 11:27; 1 Cor 11:25; 2 Cor 3:6; Heb 7–13.

how that gospel sheds light on our present subject. The redemptive and unifying power of Jesus Christ *supercedes* all divisive, identifying and boundary–setting categories: "There is no longer Jew or Greek, there is no longer slave or free, there is no longer male and female; for all of you are one in Christ Jesus" (Gal 3:28). Paul's message is built on a foundation other than punishment for transgression of the law. And yet he shares with Leviticus a deep concern about the problem of idolatry. Before leaving Leviticus it is that issue to which we turn next.

# 6

## A Price Too High

*Leviticus 20:1–27*

### LEVITICUS 20:13 (1–27)

LEVITICUS MAKES CLEAR THAT for Israel the understanding of sexual impurity is intertwined with the understanding of idolatry. Indeed, all forms of idolatry are thought of as *spiritual adultery*.[1] Thus, in ch. 20 the judgments against the Molech cult (2–5), and against consorting with mediums and wizards (6–7) occur in the same chapter with penalties for sexual violations of holiness (10–21).[2]

The sins of the first group of sexual transgressions in 20:10–16 are to be punished by death, executed by the people. The same

---

1. Milgrom, "Leviticus," 183.

2. Punishment for the sins with Molech and mediums goes beyond the death penalty in that the guilty shall be cut off from their people (כָּרֵת, *karet*: Lev 7:21 , 25, 27; 17:10; 18:29; 19:8; 20:3, 5, 6, 17–18; 22:3; 23:29; 26:30). The penalty is inflicted by God and likely is meant to involve extirpation, "the eventual total extinction of one's line, by whatever means God sees fit." See Schwartz, 257; Milgrom, "Leviticus," 162.

execution by humans was the case for those guilty of sacrifice to Molech, except that then they were also cut off by God for defiling the sanctuary and profaning God's name (3,5). This cutting off, eradication of the person's family line, is the punishment for the second group of sexual sins in 20:17–19 (perhaps implying death at God's hand as well). The third group of sins (20–21) brings childlessness.[3] Three things relative to these penalties are to be noticed from the texts.

First, Leviticus is consistent in its purpose to guard the land from suffering defilement by transmission to it of the people's sins. "You shall keep all my statutes and all my ordinances, and observe them *so that* the land to which I bring you to settle in may not vomit you out" (20:22).

Second, holiness for the people involves not being like their predecessors in the land. "You shall not follow the practices of the nation that I am driving out before you. Because they did all these things, I abhorred them" (20:23). Israel is called and expected to be distinct from other peoples. That distinction is an effect of covenant law.

Third, separation is therefore inherent in the concept of holiness, and this separation involves distinction of clean and unclean: "I am the Lord your God; I have separated you from the peoples. You shall therefore make a distinction between the clean animal and the unclean . . . you shall not bring abomination on yourselves . . . You shall be holy to me; for I the LORD am holy, and I have separated you from the other peoples to be mine" (20:24c, 25a, 26).

The purpose of separation or holiness is sometimes preserved by mitigation of the law that was given to protect holiness. So it is helpful to notice the outcome of the prescribed death penalty for these particular sins. The penalty was likely *not* utilized. Thus,

> . . . the death penalty might also merely indicate the seriousness of the crime without calling for its actual implementation in every case. In fact, there is very little evidence that many of these sanctions were ever actually

---

3. Milgrom, "Leviticus," 183; Schwartz, 256–7. Kaiser, 1142, suggests that this means being made a eunuch.

used in ancient Israel. In only one case is no commuta-
tion of the sanction ever allowed; that is in first-degree
murder. The law strictly warns, "Do not accept a ransom
for the life of a murderer, who deserves to die. He must
surely be put to death (Num 35:31 NIV). The word emphasized is רפכ (*koper*), a *"deliverance or a ransom by
means of a substitute."* Traditional wisdom, both in the
Jewish and in the Christian communities commenting
on this verse, interpreted it to mean that in the fourteen
to nineteen other cases (the count is variously given)
calling for capital punishment in the OT, it was possible to have the sentence of death commuted by some
appropriate *koper* that a judge would determine. Thus
the death penalty showed how serious the crime was,
and the provision of a substitute, either of money or of
some other reparation, allowed the individual's life to be
spared in every case, except where that individual had
not spared someone else's life by malice and forethought,
i.e., in first-degree murder.[4]

Coupled with such provision for substitutionary atonement
is the absence in the OT of any person's execution because of same
gender human sexual activity. This absence of execution and the
deliverance provided by atonement share the context of the punishment law in Leviticus 20:13. It is a context that invites careful
consideration.

---

4. Kaiser, 1142. On pollution of the land in the case of murder, and the
prohibition of ransom for said offense, see Hackett, "Numbers," 264, regarding
Num 35:30–34. Fox, 354, points out that ransom (i.e. paid to the victim's family) for murder is not allowed because murder is more than a sin against the
family: it is a pollution of the land, which in turn endangers the inhabitants of
divine wrath. Von Rad, *Theology*, 1:262–72, describes the meaning of *Sin and
Atonement* in Israel. This involves the term רפכ (*koper)* meaning, *to cover*, or
*to perform an act of atonement*. In atonement the priests act as representatives
of the LORD, the LORD acts through the priests, the animal of sacrifice bears
the sin of the person(s), and with the offering of the animal's life the act of sin
is expiated or removed along with its baneful consequences. See Rylaarsdam,
309–16.

## Summary

The texts in Leviticus 18 and 20 about same gender sexual activity are part of the Torah's instruction for ordinary people amidst everyday life in the covenant community in the land.[5] The relationship of people, land, and covenant–keeping is central to the message of Leviticus. The call to holiness is inherent in covenant and includes Israel's ethical and practical separateness from other peoples.

Jacob Milgrom has emphasized this very context and connection of people, land, and holiness. His interpretation of 18:22 and its specific mention of *lyings down* relates the sexual prohibitions to the extended family of a man living within the land that God has given, which land the man must be careful not to defile. Just as certain sexual relations are forbidden for the man with particular women in the extended family, so are corresponding males within the extended family forbidden to the man's sexual encounter. This interpretation makes good sense in the context of the instruction relayed in chapters 17–19.

Mary Douglas considers the similarity of these texts in relation to other laws to which they may logically be compared. Analogy suggests a certain consistency and an implicit order. Her study of the structure of Leviticus, chapters 18–20 in particular, leads to Douglas' focus on the theme of God's righteousness and justice in chapter 19, the center of the three–chapter trilogy.[6] The righteousness of God is in sharp contrast to other gods, and consequently God's people are not to be like other peoples. The zenith of righteousness is the simple ethical command to love the neighbor and the alien as one loves self. Like other authors to whom this present study refers, Douglas distinguishes between (1)

---

5. Our English word *Torah* comes directly transliterated from the Hebrew תּוֹרָה. The LXX normally translates the word as νόμος (*nomos*) which English translations of both OT and NT render as *law*. Canonically it encompasses the five books of the Pentateuch: Genesis–Deuteronomy. It may be helpful to understand the term as *instruction*.

6. Achtemeier, 82: "Yahweh's righteousness is his fulfillment of the demands of the relationship which exists between him and his people Israel, his fulfillment of the covenant whch he has made with his chosen nation."

homosexuality as a life-condition or orientation, and (2) same sex actions or practices. Leviticus, she maintains, has no sense of the former and therefore legislates only against the latter.

Robert Gagnon holds to the commonly accepted or traditional view of Lev 18:22 and 20:13 as absolute laws that hold true for all people within and outside the Promised Land. He emphasizes the order of creation and the complementarity or fittedness of male and female sexual partners. Holiness means keeping the categories of creation distinct and unmixed.

Gagnon sees the position of Paul in the New Testament to be a carry-over of this Leviticus view, and maintains that the two covenants (*old* and new) are in agreement on the subject of homosexuality. Gagnon thus adheres to the priority of a particular view of law as the governing factor for the community of faith, whether in the Old Testament or the New.[7]

We should not slight the presence and power of ransom, forgiveness, and atonement, in the books of the law. That a ransom could be made for the sake of covering one's sin with a guilt offering is exemplified in Lev 19:21–2. The priest thus makes atonement for the sin that was committed and the sinner is forgiven. That there was a Day of Atonement established in and for Israel (23:26) was not only a provision for the forgiveness of sin.[8] It also established a localized setting about which the people could be confident in the presence of God. The mercy seat (Lev 16:2) upon the Ark of the Covenant was where God kept appointment and promise.[9]

7. Regarding law in the OT see Anderson, 95–109; Mendenhall, "Law and Covenant," 2:26–46, and 3:49–76; Brueggemann, *Theology*, 181–201; Fretheim, *Exodus*, 21–2, 201–54; Muilenburg, *Israel*, 63–74; Von Rad, *Moses*; *Theology* 1:187–231. Regarding law in the NT see Bornkamm, *Jesus*, 96–117; Bultmann, *Theology* I:§27; Goppelt, *Theology* 2:224–229; Räisänen, *Law*; Sanders, *Paul*; Westerholm, *Israel's Law*.

8. The Hebrew, הַכִּפֻּרִים יוֹם (yôm hakkippûrîm) is rendered ἡμέρα ἐξιλασμοῦ (hēmera exilasmou) in the LXX (Lev 23:27), translated as *Day of Atonement* in NRSV (Yom Kippur); Lev 16:29–34; 23:26–32; Num 29:7–11.

9. The mercy seat, ἱλαστήριον (hilasterion) is used by Paul in Rom 3:25 to speak of Christ's sacrifice of atonement by his blood. In Ex. 25:16–17 (LXX) it is the lid of the ark of the covenant, the cover of the container of the Ten Commandments, intended as the seat on which God would meet with

No Condemnation!

The concepts of atonement and mercy seat lead us directly to the Apostle Paul. He applies these concepts to the understanding of Christ's effective work in atoning for sin and God's presence in Christ for the atoning purpose. Romans 3:21–26 reads:

> But now, apart from law, the righteousness of God has been disclosed, and is attested by the law and the prophets, the righteousness of God through faith in Jesus Christ for all who believe. For there is no distinction, since all have sinned and fall short of the glory of God; they are now justified by his grace as a gift, through the redemption that is in Christ Jesus, whom God put forward as a sacrifice of atonement by his blood, effective through faith. He did this to show his righteousness, because in his divine forbearance he had passed over the sins previously committed; it was to prove at the present time that he himself is righteous and that he justifies the one who has faith in Jesus.

---

and speak to Israel. It is the place of forgiveness. See Büchsel and Herrmann, "ἱλαστήριον, ἵλεως, κτλ.," 300–23.

# 7

# Industry and Abuse

## *1 Timothy 1:3–13 and 1 Corinthians 6:9–10*

FIRST TIMOTHY IS NOT usually attributed to Paul by most biblical scholars who mostly see it arising from later interpreters of Paul's teaching.[1] What may be called the *Undisputed Letters* (1 Thessalonians, Galatians, 1–2 Corinthians, Philippians, Romans, Philemon) are thought to have come from Paul. What may be called the *Disputed Letters* (Colossians, Ephesians, 2 Thessalonians, 1–2 Timothy, Titus) are thought to have come later from Paul's interpreters. But the authority of Paul is affirmed by these epistles, even as today's scholars and readers alike find profitable instruction, deep and lively conviction, and unplumbed depth in all the letters that bear Paul's name. Indeed, the disputed letters extend and develop much of Paul's meaning, to the nourishment of the church throughout the ages.[2]

The two texts we consider now have certain content in common. They also each have their own character and purpose. We

---

1. Roetzel, 153–160; Bassler, 2229–31.

2. Hay, "Pauline Theology After Paul," 181, 188, and speaking of the disputed letters, 195, "Their authors would have agreed with Albert Schweitzer that 'Paul is the patron-saint of thought in Christianity.'" See Schweitzer, 377.

will pay attention to both aspects of both texts, in order to appreciate the value that links as well as distinguishes them. First Timothy 1:9–10 is *both* an echo of 1 Cor 6:9–10 (which, of the two texts, was written first) *and* is significant in its own right. Our consideration is in the light of these two attributes of similarity and difference.[3]

## 1 TIMOTHY 1:9–10 (3–11)

First Timothy 1:9–10 and 1 Cor 6:9–10 share two similarities. First, the word *arsenokoites* is translated as *sodomites* in both texts (NRSV). We recall that no derivative of the name of the city of Sodom occurs in the native language of *any* biblical text. But the word is there in some English versions.[4] It is used in 1 Timothy's argument against the *lawless*, just as 1 Corinthians uses it within the argument against the *unrighteous* (or *unjust*, 6:1, 9).[5] Second, the word *arsenokoites* occurs amidst a *catalog of vices*, a common devise for castigating immorality or general characterization of sinners. Jews used such lists or catalogs with reference to Gentiles. Gentiles used vice lists for those with whom they had ethical issues or those in transgression of customs and norms. Just as lists of virtues could be used in eulogy or affirmation, so vice lists accused and sometimes painted with slurs. The content and use

---

3. Dunn, 775, says of the Pastoral Epistles, among which 1 Timothy is counted, "They helped to establish a pattern of 'the truth,' 'the faith,' and 'sound teaching' as the yardstick and bulwark by which to judge and ward off false teaching and heresy." Written by Paul or not, the letters are not to be devalued. See Dunn, 775–80.

4. The word ἀρσενοκοῖται (*arsenokoitai*), occurs only in these two texts in the New Testament. Knust, 165, says of the Greek text, ". . . the word 'sodomite' simply does not appear, and there is no reference, implicit or explicit, to the story of Sodom." We can see in these texts what Mary Douglas observed about Leviticus, that there is no indication of understanding homosexuality as a condition or orientation of being, as what is spoken against is homosexual activity by heterosexual persons.

5. 1 Tim 1:9, ἀνόμοις (*anomois*: lawless, outside the law); 1 Cor 6:9, ἄδικοι (*adikoi*: unrighteous, unjust). The terms are the antithesis of two key concepts: law, νόμος (*nomos*), and righteous, δίκαιος (*dikaios*). The antagonists are outside or in error over against these realms.

of vice lists involved broad generalities. We note that references to actual context or real people are rare; writers are not selective about content but include all the evils that people might possibly do; the longer the list, the weightier it is thought to be; it is hard to determine whether a particular point within the list is the object of the writer's use of it; the lists are, therefore, stereotypical.[6]

The use of such conventional vilification corresponds to the vague and imprecise nature of the author's attack against the false teachers. There are, however, several concrete issues relative to the opponents: they forbid marriage and advocate avoidance of certain foods (4:3); they teach that the resurrection has already happened (2 Tim 2:18); they use the profane chatter and contradictions of false knowledge (6:20).

These issues suggest attribution of the problem to an early form of Gnosticism. We also note the problems of myths and genealogies (1:4), those who desire to teach the law (1:7), and the role of women in some aspects of church life (2:9), thus making it difficult to pinpoint exactly the identity of those about whom the letter speaks.[7]

It is clear that the author gives no particular weight to the sexual terms in his vice lists or other accusations against his adversaries. But there are aspects of the 1 Timothy text that should be noted relative to our study. In 1 Tim 1:5, we learn that the author is aiming at persons whose instruction has deviated from *a pure heart, a good conscience, and sincere faith.* These persons desire to be teachers of the law but they do not understand the things of which they speak (v. 7).

*Lawlessness* then becomes the first item in the catalog of vices that proceeds from v. 9. The entire list mentions 14 vices, among which vices 10–12 are translated as *fornicators, sodomites,* and *slave traders* (v. 10).[8] These three words seem to belong together as a set

6. Nissinen, 114; Scroggs, 101–9. See vice lists in Rom 1:29–31; 1 Cor 5:10, 11; 6:9–10; 2 Cor 12:20; Gal 5:19–23; Col 3:18–4:1; Eph 5:21—6:9; 2 Tim 3:1-5.

7. Dunn, 782–3. On Gnosticism see Roetzel, 34–5.

8. Scroggs, 118, cites *pornoi, arsenokoitai, andrapodista* (πόρνοις ἀρσενοκοίταις ἀνδραποδισταῖς). Context informs a word and here the second term lends meaning to the first and third.

of indictments against what would have been a sex industry or abusive social malady. In the first term, *pornoi* (plural), *fornicators*, we can hear an echo of our word *pornography*. The *pornos* (singular), ". . . in normal Greek usage means 'male prostitute'. . ." and would seem likely to have exactly that connotation here, standing as it does in association with *arsenokoitai* (translated as *sodomites*).[9]

We shall see in our study of 1 Cor 6:9–10 that the *arsenokoites* refers to the dominant or assertive person in the male–to–male sexual encounters between adult men and boys or youthful males, that is, between the user and the used. Instead of the *pornos* in 1 Timothy, Paul speaks of the *malakos* in 1 Corinthians 6, meaning the *soft, effeminate, weaker* partner who was either forced into the relationship or sold himself into it. Such relationships were common.

That the writer of 1 Timothy had in mind the sex trade would be confirmed by his use of the third word in this set, *andrapodista*, translated as *slave trader*. The word also refers to a *kidnapper*. Kidnapping for the purpose of sale into slavery, particularly of young victims, supplied the brothel houses with both boys and girls. Scroggs summarizes this angle of textual background: "The three words would thus fit together and could be translated: 'male prostitutes, males who lie [with them], and slave–dealers [who procure them]'. . . I thus draw the conclusion that the vice list in 1 Timothy is not condemnatory of homosexuality in general, not even pederasty in general, but that specific form of pederasty which consisted of enslaving boys or youths for sexual purposes, and the use of these boys by adult males."[10]

If this constitutes the accurate sense of the 1 Timothy text then it may prompt us to examine whether it is appropriate to go beyond the meanings that the biblical author had in mind. In Paul's case, he certainly had specific problems in view when he wrote to the Corinthians, as did the author of 1 Timothy in using some of

9. Scroggs, 119; Abbott–Smith, 372–3; Hauck and Schulz, "πόρνη, πορνεύω, κτλ.," 579–84. BDAG, 693, understands the term broadly in NT literature as *sexual immorality*.

10. Scroggs, 120. The same three ideas appear in Leviticus 18 and 20, Deut 23:18 and 24:7.

the same terminology.[11] But to assume that these texts spoke of *our* concept of homosexuality is to impose our understanding onto the authors' thought. It is to read a modern concept into an ancient text.[12] Thus, ". . . Paul's words should not be used for generalizations that go beyond his experience and world."[13] It follows that trying to understand an author like Paul, on his own terms and in his own time, is one step in the journey of appreciating Scripture and its power today.

## CORINTHIANS 6:9-10 (1-20)

Paul has previously addressed a problem of church discipline in regard to a sexual matter, in 5:1–13. In that case a man was *living with his father's wife*. The woman was, presumably, the man's stepmother, as Paul does not refer to the situation as incest. She must have been either widowed or divorced from the man's father, as Paul does not refer to the situation as adultery. He calls it *fornication*, and it is a practice forbidden in Lev 18:8 and 20:11, where the transgression is deemed a capital offense and requires the death penalty.[14]

11. Dunn, 791, sees the list of examples of what is lawless and profane, beginning in v. 9b, extended in 9c and v. 10 into a list of transgressions against the second table of the law. Are these, therefore, to be understood as adultery?

12. In a related way Paul cautions the Corinthians (1 Cor 4:6) not to go *beyond what is written*. This may refer to the scriptural passages that have been cited in 1 Corinthians 1–3, if not to the entirety of (OT) Scripture, which should not be exceeded with beliefs or interpretations of one's own; Barrett, 106–7; Hooker, "Beyond the Things that are Written," 295–309.

13. Nissinen, 118, suggests that the sexual terminology of both the Corinthians and Timothy texts is too vague to venture more than an educated guess at the meaning: "Regardless of the kind of sexuality meant in 1 Corinthians 6:9 and 1 Timothy 1:10, in their current contexts they are examples of the exploitation of persons. This is the hermeneutical horizon for understanding the individual components of the lists of vices. What Paul primarily opposes is the wrong that people do to others."

14. Barrett, 120–1. Paul uses the word *porneia*, in 1 Cor 5:1, (the root of our word, "pornography") translated as "fornication" by Barrett, or "sexual immorality" in the NRSV. D. Wright, "Leviticus," 168, indicates that especially in the context of sexual prohibitions, as in Leviticus 18 and 20, 'nakedness' refers specifically to the genitals and "to *uncover nakedness* was a euphemism

Paul returns to sexual matters in 6:12 and ch. 7. Among some of the Corinthian Christians there may have been a view that in faith one should refrain from sexual relations within marriage. Thus, the NRSV has put quotation marks around 7:1b: "It is well for a man not to touch a woman." Paul is here quoting something that was said by some of the Corinthians as he sets out to answer what they have written to him.[15] Furthermore, it may have been the case that some who thought marriage should be spared all carnal activity also thought that the husband could therefore find sexual relief outside of marriage:

> Schlatter may well be right in connecting the implied claim to the right to make use of a harlot with the Corinthian attitude to marriage which appears in chapter vii—marriage is to be avoided if possible, and married people would do well to avoid intercourse. It could have been argued in Corinth (especially, Schlatter suggests, by Christian women) that the right course was for a husband to keep his wife pure, and, if necessary, find occasional sexual satisfaction in a harlot.[16]

This course of action would be justified with the quotation in 6:12, "All things are lawful for me." Then 6:15–16 would be Paul's contradiction of such an attitude and practice: "Do you not know that your bodies are members of Christ? Should I therefore take the members of Christ and make them members of a prostitute? Never! Do you not know that whoever is united to a prostitute becomes one body with her?"

In 6:9–11 Paul turns to reflection upon the past lives of some of the Corinthians. The *unrighteous* or *unjust* in v. 9 (*wrongdoers* in the NRSV) points back to v. 8, where Paul holds the mirror of their own wrongdoing against one another before his readers' eyes.[17] He

---

for sexual intercourse." See Harper's in–depth study of this term in, *Porneia,* especially 375–83.

15. Furnish, 32; Barrett, 154: "Some difficulty is alleviated if these words are regarded as a quotation from the Corinthian letter . . ."

16. Barrett, 145.

17. ἄδικοι (*adikoi*) is the antithesis of 'just/righteous' (*dikaios*). Barrett,

echoes Rom 2:1 (*therefore you have no excuse . . . when you judge others . . . because you, the judge, are doing the very same things*). He anticipates 1 Cor 6:11 (*And this is what some of you used to be*). He therefore will not allow the unrighteousness of some to feed the self–righteousness of others. In any case, the context here is of utmost importance for our understanding of specific verses.

Paul begins ch. 6 by addressing Christians' mutual litigation: ". . . do you dare to take it to court before the unrighteous . . . is no one among you wise enough to decide between one believer and another? . . . to have lawsuits at all with one another is already a defeat for you." (1, 5, 7). Thus runs his chief concern throughout this portion of the epistle, and Paul illustrates what he means in ch. 6 with three sets of examples that reach back into ch. 5. Each list of examples is successively expanded onto the next. All are forms of exploitative wrong–doing: immoral, greedy, robbers, idolaters (5:10); sexually immoral, greedy, idolater, reviler, drunkard, robber (5:11); fornicators, idolaters, adulterers, male prostitutes, sodomites, thieves, the greedy, drunkards, revilers, robbers (6:9–10).

Paul illustrates what he means by wrongdoing or unrighteousness with a list of behaviors in 6:9–10.[18] Two unusual nouns occur in v. 9. First, the NRSV translates as *male prostitutes* what is a single word in the Greek text.[19] Barrett uses the term *catamites*. It indicates *soft, weak, effeminate*, and had three probable points of reference: (1) pederasty was considered among the Greeks as an important aspect of a young boy's education; (2) young slave boys were often exploited by older men for sexual gratification; (3) sex–for–sale was common among call–boys used by older men. The word implicitly points to a young person and refers to the passive

---

139: "It is not only the New Testament that contains teaching of this kind . . . Greek moral philosophy too was not unaware that it was better to suffer evil than to do it."

18. Paul's list may relate to observations of life in Corinth and a catalog of vices named in the traditions of Hellenistic Judaism; Barrett, 140; Braun, "πλανάω, πλάνη, κτλ.," 244; Conzelmann, 106.

19. For μαλακοί (*malakoi*) see Nissinen, 113–19; Fitzmyer, *First Corinthians*, 255–8.

partner in male–to–male sexual relations. It involved power and dominance or pay and (male) prostitution.[20]

Second, the word translated as *sodomites*, is made of two words, *male* and *one who goes to bed* (here a euphemism for sexual intercourse; see Rom 13:13, where *koitais* is translated as *licentiousness* and refers to sexual excesses).[21] The two words that form the single Greek term in v. 9 may be an echo of Lev 18:22 and 20:13, (*arsenos* and *koimethe, koiten*) according to its Greek version.[22] We remember that this Greek translation of the Old Testament was, for the most part, the Bible of the NT authors. The word, *sodomites*, in 1 Cor 6. 9, is in apposition to *male prostitutes*, and indicates the active role in male–to–male sexual relations, hence, the senior, powerful, or purchasing partner.[23]

Paul thus addresses the problem of sexual trafficking either for pay or as a power field in which one person dominated another. Because the practice of male–to–male sex was a common occurrence in the Gentile world of Paul's time, these terms were parts of a traditional list of various vices commonly attributed by Jews to Gentiles. It is not only that these are old ways of life that Paul says the believers in Christ should now put behind them. More than that, Paul here proclaims the good news of redemption, "addressing the greatest of miracles, a church of redeemed sinners, won from their old life by the power of God."[24]

---

20. Barrett, 140; Furnish, 58–60; Tiede, 151.

21. For ἀρσενοκοῖται (*arsenokoitai*) see Fitzmyer, *1 Corinthians*, 256–7, who says that the term should *not* be translated as *homosexual*, a modern term for one's sexual orientation as well as activity, and which came into use in the 19th century to denote a person's sexual preference for another person of the same sex.

22. Nissinen, 116. The reference is to the Septuagint (LXX), which translation renders the two Leviticus texts in the way usually understood today, and some think perhaps also by Paul.

23. Tiede, 150: "The text was not speaking about men with feminine mannerisms or men with same–sex affections, but about men who used other men for coitus . . . The text does not speak to the question of homosexual orientation. This text only speaks literally about a behavior between males."

24. Barrett, 140–1.

## Summary

Throughout the various phases of our study and relative to the biblical texts correspondingly involved it remains important for us to ask, "What is Paul (or Genesis, or Leviticus) really against?" Homosexuality, as an orientation in life, is not part of the context and is not involved in Paul's thinking in these passages.[25] We may also note that even the prohibited sexual activities are not referred to as *sins* but rather as vices symptomatic of the *power and force* of sin. The vices are symptomatic of life outside of faith in Christ. The vices, therefore, of which Paul speaks were for him illustrations of something bigger, namely alienation and exclusion from the covenant, from the faith community, and from allegiance to Christ.

First Timothy 1 seems particularly focused on such life as an industry or trade, in which human dignity is trampled, promiscuity is practiced, and profit is a prime motive. First Corinthians 6 is likely also focused on the widely practiced institution of Gentile culture and society that assumed the sexual use of young men or boys by older men, including men who were married and heterosexual but nevertheless who used young male lovers. The message is thus amazingly pertinent for challenging the pernicious problem of the sex industry, sex trafficking, and sexual exploitation in today's world.

We are reminded that Paul takes the violation of normal roles to be forms of unrighteousness illustrative of the idolatry of

---

25. Akenson, 12–13, comments on the suggestion that, "just possibly, Saul is not really against homosexuality but against sexual acts in which at least one of the males has to behave like a woman (that is, be a passive recipient) or in which a woman may behave like a man, with another woman. That goes out the window, however, when one notes the word Saul uses for dominant men who have sexual congress with passive males—a mode of sexual intercourse in which the supposedly natural dominance of the male is preserved. These men are called *arsenokoitai* (1 Cor. 6:9). Generation after generation of translators have tried to paraphrase this term, for it is one of extreme derogation. It means butt–fuckers, and the apostle will have none of it. Despite the tenor of his times, Saul was unabashedly homophobic and, as *The Guardian* deftly noted, 'not much liked by the gay lobby, right?' (*Guardian*, 11 September 1997)." We note that Akenson's blunt assessment points to Paul as part of the problem ("unabashedly homophobic"), if not the whole of it. Tiede's essay in its entirety is helpful here.

the Gentile world. Such practices were likely considered *unclean*. But to name and castigate such offenses was for Paul not an end in itself, but rather a means to an end. The true purpose for him remained always to illustrate and emphasize the far–reaching and all–encompassing effect of God's redemption in Christ. Furthermore, those who enter and enjoy this redemption do so on the sole basis of faith in Christ alone.

Paul seems always to have in mind the big picture of sin as the force that drives a wedge between humans and God.[26] It is God's righteousness and redemption wrought in Christ that removes that wedge and enables the relationship of obedience and trust. Redemption in Christ brings a life that is unmistakably new and scandalously inclusive: "So if *anyone* is in Christ, there is a new creation: everything old has passed away; see, everything has become new . . . that is, in Christ God was reconciling the world to himself, not counting their trespasses against them, and entrusting the message of reconciliation to us" (2 Cor 5:17–19).

The new life in Christ of which Paul here speaks is not only that which he has received for himself. It is not only that of the apostles. It is that which belongs to *all* who have come to share in the saving event of God's work in Christ. Such persons are *in Christ*, reconciled to God through Christ and thus part of the *new creation*.[27]

The new life in the new creation is for all who have been joined to Christ in baptism (Gal 3:26–8).[28] They are convinced

---

26. Rom 7:8, 11 speak of sin (singular) as a force or power, fierce and strong enough to seize hold of the commandment of law, and use that commandment to increase in a person the very thing against which the commandment legislates! This is the predicament outside of Christ, well beyond the human will to manage or change. The various vices in Paul's lists are symptoms illustrative of this state of being in the old life, the life of sin or of the flesh.

27. Bultmann, *Second Corinthians*, 156–8.

28. See the splendid essay by Gaiser, "A New Word." His analysis of Isaiah 56 argues, (1) *by analogy*: eunuchs once banned from altar and assembly are welcome in God's new community of outcasts; (2) *by eschatological confidence*: the law–ban is overturned by the law–giver as the LORD builds the new community; (3) *by radical extension* of grace, whereby all people, heterosexual and homosexual alike, play by the same rules, rely on gift, and live in covenantal responsibility.

that Christ has died for all, and therefore they too have died (2 Cor 5:14).[29] They have died in relation to sin (Rom 6:1–12), in relation to the law (Rom 7:4; Gal 2:19), and in relation to the world (Gal 6:14). They thus no longer live for themselves, but for him who for their sakes died and was raised (2 Cor 5:15).

29. See Moule; Schweizer; Tannehill.

# 8

## The Big Bad Bargain

*Romans 1:16–32*

### RIGHTEOUSNESS AND WRATH

PAUL'S MESSAGE IN ROMANS begins with two key themes that will inform the content of the entire epistle. The themes are *righteousness* and *wrath*. The theme of *righteousness* is introduced in 1:16–17, as Paul says that *the gospel is the power of God for salvation to everyone who has faith*. He next proclaims that in *it* (the gospel) *the righteousness of God is revealed through faith for faith*.[1] The theme of *the wrath of God* is introduced in 1:18, as Paul speaks also of whence that wrath has come: *the wrath of God is revealed from heaven against all ungodliness*.[2]

---

1. Moulton and Geden, 218. For δικαιοσύνη (*dikaiosynē, righteousness, justice*) in Romans, see 1:17; 3:5, 21, 22, 25, 26; 4:3, 5, 6, 9, 11, 13, 22; 5:17, 21; 6:13, 16, 18, 19, 20; 8:10; 9:30, 31; 10:3, 4, 5, 6, 10; 14:17.

2. Ibid., 703, list the Romans passages with ὀργὴ or ὀργὴ θεοῦ (*orgē theou, wrath of God*): 1:18; 2:5, 8; 3:5; 4:15; 5:9; 9:22; 12:19; 13:4, 5. It is *divine* wrath. Against whom does God's wrath militate? Elliot, 79, responds: "My answer is

*The righteousness of God* as we meet it in Romans (and, through Paul, as it is rooted in the Hebrew tradition) has to do with the way in which God acts, and particularly the way God acts in making and maintaining covenant.[3] God's righteousness is God's activity and according to 1:16–17 it is power active in the gospel.[4] "The gospel is both the power of God leading to salvation for every believer, and also the site of revelation of God's righteousness."[5]

Paul in Romans thus speaks of divine righteousness as God's active, covenant–maintaining power that generates new life. We note that, (1) the NRSV translates Rom 3:5 as *justice*, emphasizing that human injustice does not nullify the righteousness/justice of God as a given, a gift; (2) Rom 3:21 echoes 1:16, in locating the righteousness of God in its disclosure in faith in Jesus Christ; (3) Rom 4:3 quotes Gen 15:6, heralding Abraham's faith as reckoned or counted to him as righteousness, which same righteousness is also counted to us in faith, Rom 5:1. God's power is not only gift, but is generatively faith–producing.[6]

---

that Paul intends his hearers to recognize definite allusions to none other than *the Caesars themselves*. No others would serve Paul's argument so effectively by offering, in their own persons, a fitting lesson on the inevitability with which divine punishment follows horrendous crimes." Gaius Caligula and Nero fit the worst descriptions of such cases and are proximate to Paul's time. See Nanos, 256, who acknowledges the depraved behavior of these same two Caesars.

3. Thus we find the narrative of covenant righteousness as we see it unfolding in Gen 15:6; 18:19; Deut 6:25; praised in Psa 11:7; proclaimed in Isa 45:8, 23–4, among many other texts.

4. Hultgren, *Romans*, 613, "Theological priority must be given not to the human plight before God (the 'anthropological' approach) but to God, a God who seeks to restore a relationship with rebellious humanity (the 'theological' approach). The gospel reveals the 'righteousness of God' that has been manifested, even exercised, by God in Christ."

5. Ziesler, 186–7; G. Wright, 53, 59, points out that the basis for the biblical story and biblical theology is not about the attributes of God but the activity of God and "to inquire further as to what portions of the Biblical recital of Divine activity in history are the most important" (59) leads us to the cross: ". . . the Cross is the only adequate symbol of Biblical faith, since in it the righteousness of God is truly presented in both its aspects of judgment and of salvation, as also man's sin and redemption." (91).

6. Schrenk, 206, speaks of the righteousness of God as "a justifying action

*God's wrath* denotes divine reaction to human sin and evil. It is linked to monotheism and covenant with God. It is not "an irrational or irresponsible outburst of rage" nor does it indicate an angry deity who must be placated. God's wrath signifies "the justifiable reaction of a loving and faithful God toward his disobedient people and their proneness to idolatry, to evil, and to sinful conduct."[7] That the wrath of God is revealed *from heaven* speaks of divine ownership and inevitability.[8] That the wrath of God is revealed against *all* ungodliness speaks of its inclusiveness and inescapability.[9] That the wrath of God is revealed against those who suppress the truth by their *wickedness* speaks of its service to righteousness.[10] Three examples of Paul's use of the term *wrath* in Romans are helpful.

First, Rom 2:5 reads, "But by your hard and impenitent heart you are storing up wrath for yourself on the day of wrath, when God's righteous judgment will be revealed." Wrath here is future, and speaks of the last day, the day of judgment, the day of wrath.

---

of God which seizes the individual." Käsemann, 29, says that it, ". . . brings back the fallen world into the sphere of his legitimate claim . . ."

7. Fitzmyer, *Romans*, 103. Luther, *Romans*, 17, ". . . only the gospel reveals the righteousness of God . . ."

8. The modifiers of wrath, *of God* and *from heaven*, indicate monotheism: if there is only one true God then that God is responsible for all that happens "to his people and his creation, good or evil." So Fitzmyer, *Romans*, 108. See Isa 45:7; Amos 3:6.

9. Beginning with v. 18 Paul is likely addressing the situation of the Gentiles, and yet the *all* (πᾶσαν, *pasan*) here points to the cosmic extension of God's wrath. So Käsemann, 38: "The whole world even in its secularity belongs to the Creator." Moxnes, 35, speaking of God's impartiality, says, "As a whole Rom 1:18—3:20 resembles the judgment speeches by the Old Testament prophets, especially by Amos. Every Jew would agree with Paul's pronunciation of judgment on the godless Gentiles, 1:18–32, but then he turns around and directs his accusation against Israel. It is on this note that he starts the dialogue in 2:1 . . ." See Amos 1:1—2:3; 2:4–5.

10. Both words, righteousness and wickedness (literally: injustice, unrighteousness) are formed on the same (δικ-, *dik-*) root, in the case of unrighteousness with the negative prefix (α-, *a-*) to show opposition or absence; hence, *dikaios* (righteous) as over against *adikos* (unrighteous).

Thus, it is not only a presently operative force, but a future expectation and certainty.

Second, Rom 3:5 reads, "But if our injustice serves to confirm the justice of God, what should we say? That God is unjust to inflict wrath on us?" It is *God's* wrath, God's response and responsibility, a disposition of the one and only true God, whose will is free and prevalent.

Third, Rom 4:15 reads, "For the law brings wrath." Righteousness is revealed in the gospel. Wrath is exercised in the law. God's wrath is effective towards "the human condition apart from the influence of the preached gospel (1:18—3:20)."[11] Wrath involves all humanity, "humanity as such and not just representatives of religious groupings."[12] Thus, "Paul looks at the 'totality of the cosmos' when it is left to itself without the gospel . . . without the gospel affecting their lives all humanity is sinful and estranged from God. As a result his wrath is manifested toward them all."[13]

Paul speaks of wrath *after* having spoken of righteousness when he articulates these two key parts to his message. We note straightaway that in the gospel the righteousness of God is revealed (1:17), all are now justified by God's grace as a gift, and this comes through the redemption that is in Christ Jesus (3:24). Then we note that the wrath of God is revealed against all ungodliness (1:18) and all have sinned and fall short of the glory of God (3:23). Paul thus simultaneously answers the *who* question, informed by the themes of righteousness and wrath: *who* is everyone! All

---

11. Fitzmyer, *Romans*, 269; Stählin, 443: ". . . the wrath of God works . . . so that the doer's act falls on his own head." Käsemann, 48, "Despisers of God bring down God's curse on themselves."

12. Käsemann, 33. Barth, 42, "The wrath of God is the judgement under which we stand in so far as we do not love the Judge; it is the, 'No' which meets us when we do not affirm it; it is the protest pronounced always and everywhere against the course of the world in so far as we we do not accept the protest as our own . . ."

13. Fitzmyer, *Romans*, 270. Hultgren, *Romans*, 85, speaking of Paul's indictment against the entire world, "He establishes that all persons, Jew and Gentile alike, are under the power of sin (3:9)."

humanity is encompassed in the inclusive categories of Jew and Gentile.[14]

Although he has not named Greeks or Gentiles in ch. 1, it does become clear from 2:1 onwards, or certainly from 2:9 and following, that he had been thinking of Gentiles in ch. 1 and Jews thereafter. The distinction, therefore, between Jew and non–Jew is no longer synonymous with insider–outsider. With the coming of Christ for *all*, the basis for inclusion in the covenant and kingdom has changed, even as *all* are in need of the Christ who has come for them.

Paul has already sounded the theme of inclusiveness through redemption in Christ in Rom 1:16. There he announced, "For I am not ashamed of the gospel; it is the power of God for salvation to *everyone* who has faith, to the Jew first and also to the Greek." We could read Rom 1:16 with this emphasis: ". . . *it* is the power of God for salvation." *It* refers to the gospel. *It*, and no other power, is the effective power for salvation. Furthermore, Paul says of *it*, the gospel, "For in it the righteousness of God is revealed through faith for faith . . ." (1:17).

*Righteousness* speaks of God's saving relationship with people, and God's people in relation to others and among themselves. *Righteousness* involves the norms of the relationship and behavior within the relationship. It thus relates to the attributes of covenant with God, including for Israel awareness of God, consciousness of self, worship, justice, law, social relationships, history and nationhood, based in what the Lord has done and is doing. Righteousness includes the double sense of (1) individual covenant loyalty towards God and towards the community, and (2) corporate responsibility towards God on the part of the covenant community.[15]

The gift of righteousness through Christ is the message Paul drives home throughout the epistle. It is "the righteousness of God through faith in Jesus Christ for all who believe." (Rom 3:22). So

---

14. Fitzmyer, *Romans*, 256. Dodd, *Romans*, 19, "The moral universe is one; good is good and evil is evil, among Jews and Gentiles alike. The Law, rightly understood, gives a knowledge of good and evil. But in doing so it reveals a standard of goodness beyond human attainment . . . The blessing of God must be, not a recognition of goodness achieved, but a means of achieving it."

15. Ziesler, 38–44.

Paul proclaims how the right relationship with God and with the neighbor is born: accomplished through Christ, carried in the gospel, received by faith, and practiced in love. Thus, if *everyone* is to share in the gift then *everyone* also shares in the need for the gift (v. 23). Paul aims at both groups of people who comprise *everyone*. He addresses Gentiles in 1:18–32. He speaks to his fellow Jews in 2:1—3:20.[16] Romans 1:18—3:20 is a presentation of the cosmic scope of solution and problem, relevant to both Jew and Gentile.[17] Paul's gospel is news for *everyone*, although 1:18–31 likely relates specifically to the Gentile world.[18] Paul illustrates the Gentiles' need for Christ with examples from Gentiles' own practiced way of life.[19]

Two verses from this rich context have often been singled out as a stand–alone argument against homosexuality.[20] *"For this reason God gave them up to degrading passions. Their women exchanged natural intercourse for unnatural and in the same way also the men, giving up natural intercourse with women, were consumed with passion for one another"* (Rom 1:26–7).

16. Dodd, *Romans*, 18, understands 1:18—3:20 as "preliminary to the working out of the main theme" of the epistle. Käsemann, 33–34, says: "This section of the epistle speaks of human guilt and divine judgment in relation to Gentiles and Jews, who are viewed as representatives of humanity and together define the nature of the cosmos. This is why the two subsections 1:18–32 and 2:1—3:20 overlap." Paul's concern is "to depict the world under the wrath of God." The relevance for the epistle follows: "In fact the presupposition of all that is to come is given here."

17. The word order here is deliberate: solution–problem. See Sanders, 150–51.

18. Scroggs, 110–111, argues that 1:18–32 is "Paul's real story of the universal fall" in which both Jews and Gentiles are included. If 1:23 were to be understood as relating to the golden calf episode (Ps 106:19–20), then Israel's idolatry is implicated in Romans.

19. Scroggs, 113–114. We note his word, *illustration*, as over against a more dogmatic term.

20. Furnish, 81: ". . . one must remember that 1:18—3:20 is itself prefatory to the good news about the reality of God's grace, which is expounded in the rest of Romans. Romans 5:6–11 is one classic summary of Paul's gospel: While we were still 'weak', still 'sinners', and still 'enemies' of God, He reconciled us to himself through the love revealed and made real for us in Christ's death."

We have seen that these two verses are part of a context in which Paul argues that, (1) all have sinned, 3:23; (2) the right relationship with God (justification) is a gift of grace; (3) grace is given through the redemption wrought by Christ; (4) redemption is effective through faith, 3:24.

Thus, Christ has come for all because all are in need of Christ. This is Paul's main theme. The two verses now under our consideration, 1:26-7, are ancillary to that theme by proportion and thematic context. Paul's chief concern here is theological and evangelical, not ethical and moral.[21] He drives at, and is driven by, salvation in Christ for all people because all people are in need of that salvation.[22] Accordingly, Scroggs comments:

> The overarching theme of Paul in Romans is the justice and mercy of God as revealed from the perspective of the Christ event. The ultimate goal of his theme is 11:32: "For God has shut up all people into disobedience that he may have mercy upon all." The penultimate goal, however, is 3:19b: "That every mouth may be silenced and the entire world held accountable to God." The argument could be summarized in one sentence: Since the entire world, both Jew and Gentile, is guilty of sin, grace (salvation) is entirely God's gift and extends equally to Jew and Gentile.[23]

We cannot overstate the importance of recognizing Paul's essential and purposeful argument in this section of Romans. The gift of salvation for all people and the need of all people for that salvation are the tandem components of Paul's saving message. Signs or illustrations of the need for salvation, according to Paul, include the Gentile world's proclivity for unnatural sexual practices (1:26-7)

21. Friedrich, "κήρυγμα, κτλ.," 716, says that *kērygma* relates to actual proclamation (of the Christian message) as well as the result affected by proclamation.

22. Sanders, 150, argues that ". . . Paul thought from solution to plight rather than from plight to solution." Sanders says (151) that Paul's beginning point was not that all are under sin and so all need salvation, but rather, "that all must have been under sin, since God sent his son to save all equally." Hence, that all are sinful is derived from the prior conviction that Christ came for and died for all.

23. Scroggs, 110.

as well as the presumptuous and hard-hearted pronouncement of judgment upon the Gentiles, presumably by Jews (2:1).

The importance and meaning of Rom 1:26–7 rest more in the part they have in the whole argument Paul is making about idolatry and grace, rather than simply in the content of the two verses themselves. The immediate context in which 1:26–7 are situated uses cause and effect language to express the connection between two actions (one human, the other divine). Three pairs of phrases play these two actions against one another. The human action is expressed with the words, *they exchanged*. The divine action is expressed with the words, *God gave them up*. The divine action, *God gave them up*, is the effect, the cause of which is the human action, *they exchanged*.

Thus, in the first pair of phrases, the *cause* in v. 23 states: "and *they exchanged* the glory of the immortal God for images resembling a mortal human being or birds or four-footed animals or reptiles." The *effect* follows in v. 24: "Therefore *God gave them up* in the lusts of their hearts to impurity, to the degrading of their bodies among themselves."

So also, in the second pair of phrases, the *cause* in v. 25 states: "because *they exchanged* the truth about God for a lie and worshiped and served the creature rather than the Creator, who is blessed forever! Amen." And the *effect* follows in v. 26: "For this reason *God gave them up* to degrading passions."

Finally, in the third pair of phrases, the *cause* in vv. 26b–28a states: "Their women *exchanged* natural intercourse for unnatural, and in the same way also the men, giving up natural intercourse with women, were consumed with passion for one another. Men committed shameless acts with men and received in their own persons the due penalty for their error. And since they did not see fit to acknowledge God . . ." Again this is followed by the *effect* in v. 28b: ". . . *God gave them up* to a debased mind and to things that should not be done."

We note the similarity of, *they did not see fit to acknowledge God* in v. 28, and *they did not honor him as God* in v. 21. The argument comes full circle in returning to the problem of idolatry, of which the various conditions between these parts of v. 21 and v. 28 are evidence or illustrations.

We remember that Paul's argument generally, and vv. 26–7 in particular, does not mention *homosexuality* or *homosexuals*. We also remember that it is easy for us to impose our own understanding of any subject back onto previous occasions, authors, and literature. A close reading of the text is in order, with attention to particular words and themes, as we heed the evangelical story line and theological argument that Paul lays out for us. We focus on the human action first, that is, the cause. This is the fundamental sin involved in the exchange of honoring God for the falsehood of idolatry, a very bad bargain indeed!

## THEY EXCHANGED

We will give considerable attention to, *"God gave them up"* (Rom 1:24–8) in the next chapter of our study. But we now explore the human action signified by, *"they exchanged."* The two phrases, representing human action on the one hand and divine action on the other, are connected by the cause and effect relationship in which they stand in the text. Hultgren speaks of the historical and literary context of this textual material, noting that overt homosexual practice in the Greco–Roman world was common, public, and tolerated. He cites four well–documented phenomena.

First, pederasty is, "an erotic relationship of an older man with a youth . . . homosexual activity between partners of the same age category is virtually unknown in the sources." This abuse involved a differential of power and age. Second, sexual abuse of slaves by their owners was also common. This abuse was based on "a differential of power and social class." Third, there was both male and female prostitution. Fourth, the Gentile literature of Paul's time spoke of female as well as male homosexual activity.[24]

---

24. Hultgren, "Being Faithful to the Scriptures," 315–24, esecially 316. The verbs, *exchanged* (*āllaxan*) and *gave over* (*paredoken*), are past tense, showing accomplished fact. See Scroggs; Dover; Karlin regarding the Gentile literature about homosexual activity.

It was likely pederasty that Paul had in mind when he wrote 1 Cor 6:9. Jewish writers before and during Paul's time, and some Gentile writers as well, condemned the practice of pederasty. The Jews, in particular thought, "that the Gentile nations are filled with pederasts."[25] Consideration of the context of Rom 1:24–8 allows several exegetical observations. In terms of the text's *literary* context Hultgren says:

> It appears in a section running from 1:18 through 3:20 in which Paul indicts the whole world, made up of Jews and gentiles, declaring that it is under the wrath of God. In 1:18–32 Paul speaks specifically of gentiles. He starts out in verses 18 through 22 to say that the gentiles have always been capable of knowing and worshiping God, but they have refused to do so. Verses 1:23 through 32 have a structure built around the verbs of "exchange" on the part of human beings and the verbs of "giving over" (or "abandoning") on the part of God: Humanity *exchanged* . . . the glory of God for images (1:23). Therefore God *gave over* . . . humanity to impurity, to dishonoring their bodies (1:24). Humanity *exchanged* . . . the worship of God for idolatry (1:25). Therefore God *gave over* . . . humanity to dishonorable passions (1:26a). Humanity *exchanged* . . . natural relations for unnatural (1:26b–27). Since people did not acknowledge God, God *gave* them *over* . . . to a base mind and improper conduct (1:28).[26]

We may note a number of observations regarding what these texts represent. First, in Romans 1 Paul is speaking of the Gentiles who have refused to worship God and he speaks of them as a whole. He is *not* focused on individual persons. He is not discussing a small minority segment of the general population. He is not making a case against particular persons in the church. The word *they* indicates the pagan Gentile culture and their ethos as a whole.[27]

Second, Paul's use of the verb, *exchanged*, is aorist tense, like our English past tense. It relates to something that happened

25. Hultgren, "Scriptures," 317.

26. Ibid., 318.

27. This is part of a standard Jewish characterization of Gentiles.

previously, and defines it as an accomplished fact of the present time. Thus, the *exchange* happened earlier in the formation of Gentile life, and is indicative for that whole people, who are now rooted in it and it in them as a regular part of Gentile life. The root meaning of *exchanged* is *to make otherwise*, but when used as a transitive verb, taking an object, the sense is *alter or change*. Then the thing changed is named or implied, as in the accusation against Paul and Jesus, to "change *the customs* that Moses handed on to us" (Acts 6:14). Similarly the sense can be *to give (or take) in exchange* when one thing is given over or taken in exchange for something else, as we have here in Rom 1:23 (and 24, 25, 26). Here Paul refers to Ps 106:20.[28] The Psalmist, speaking of the golden calf incident during the exodus journey (Exodus 32), says of the Israelites: "They made a calf at Horeb and worshiped a cast image. They exchanged the glory of God for the image of an ox that eats grass."[29]

Third, there was something to which the Israelites once had access, the glory of God, and they exchanged that glory for something else, a metal object! This deliberate act and decision of choice came about because, "They forgot God, their Savior, who had done great things in Egypt, wondrous works in the land of Ham, and awesome deeds by the Red Sea" (Ps 106:21-2). As in Rom 1:23-8, there is a divine action of consequence to what actions people have taken: "Therefore he said he would destroy them—had not Moses, his chosen one, stood in the breach before him, to turn away his wrath from destroying them" (Ps 106:23).[30]

28. Fitzmyer, *Romans*, 283, "Paul echoes Ps 106:20, 'They exchanged their glory for the image of a grass-eating bullock', which alludes to the worship of the golden calf at Sinai (Exod 32:1-34). This rather clear allusion to the golden calf makes highly unlikely an implicit allusion to the Adam narratives . . . Although Paul alludes to an incident in Israel's history, it becomes for him an example of what happens to the world without the gospel; so he can apply the idea even to pagans."

29. Büchsel. "ἀλλάσσω, μεταλλάσσω, κτλ.," 251. Psalm 105:20 in LXX is 106:20 in English. See also Jer 2:11. Käsemann, 45, "Obviously expressed here, in traditional Jewish polemic . . . is abhorrence of Gentile idolatry."

30. We note Moses' intercession and offering of himself in the peoples' stead if God's forgiveness is not forthcoming: Exod 32:30-32 ("blot me out of

Fourth, the correspondence of the Psalm material to the Romans passage is striking: the effect on worship, forgetting God and God's works, God's intended action of response, and the intervention of God's chosen one due to the Israelites' loss of faith, all specifically mentioned in the Psalm, are mirrored in the formation of Paul's argument in Romans for how God has related to the Gentiles similarly as to the Israelites. The Gentiles *exchanged*, God *gave them up*; all have sinned and fall short of the glory of God (and now) ". . . the gospel . . . is the power of God for salvation to everyone who has faith, to the Jew first and also to the Greek" (1:16). Here is Paul's case for the assignation of all people under the rule of sin, so in need of God's grace in Christ, entering salvation in the same way through faith, that faith being the ground for righteousness for all who believe in Christ Jesus (3:22). Paul speaks of the Gentiles' *exchange* as a deliberate action that forsakes something they once had or knew but lost by their own choice: they knew God but did not honor him as God (1:19–21). "The refusal to *honor* (lit. 'glorify') God *as God* is humanity's root sin, the source of the human dilemma . . ."[31]

Fifth, in Romans 1 Paul is not speaking about homosexual attraction or orientation, but about actions that have progressed from Gentiles' deliberate choices of intentionally leaving heterosexual practices.[32]

Sixth, the transgression of limits and boundaries is indicated by the use of the verb *inflamed* or *consumed* in v. 27. What is involved is not only something beyond human normal sexual desire, but rather a raging lust that destroys the self and leads to abusive behavior. A common form of such abuse was pederasty, the use of younger boys by older men for sexual gratification. The same fact is likely what Paul addresses in 1 Cor 6:9. This is the way that

the book that you have written"). Greenstein, 139: "That the names of those who are to live is recorded on high is an ancient Near Eastern tradition; cf.. Ps 69.28; Isa 4.3; Mal 3.16; also cf. Num 11.15."

31. Keck, 2117. See Scroggs.

32. Hultgren, "Scriptures," 319: "The concept of sexual orientation, including homosexual orientation, had to wait another nineteen centuries to be formulated." Keck, 2117; Elliot, 78.

Luther understood the Corinthians text in his 1522 translation of the New Testament.[33]

Seventh, Paul therefore argues that the horrible practices of abuse must come to an end: victimizing the young or weak in society, and the spilling over of lust that manifests itself in leaving of normal heterosexual relations. Indeed, God has given over or abandoned such things to his wrath, to the dishonoring of their bodies and to the baseness of mind of those who practice such things.

Eighth, *given over* anticipates Rom 11:32.[34] The evangelical news of God's victory over sin is the end or goal, for which the means is the declaration of all as sinful: "For God has imprisoned all in disobedience so that he may be merciful to all."[35] The purpose clause, with *so that*, distinguishes the means (*imprisoned all in disobedience*) from the end (*be merciful to all*).[36] Of this "joyful and comforting summary," Karl Barth says,

> Here it is that we encounter the hidden, unknown, incomprehensible God, to whom nothing is impossible, the Lord, who is as such our Father in Jesus Christ. Here is the possibility of God pressing upon us, vastly nigh at hand, vastly rich, but also vastly beyond our understanding. Here is Beginning and End, the road and the goal of the thought of God. Here is the object of faith, which may never be depressed to an 'object'. Here is the

33. Luther's German translation of 1 Cor 6:9–10 uses, *Knabenschänder* (*pederasts*); Hultgren, "Scriptures," 317.

34. Black, 149, says that the literal meaning of the verb *imprison* is generally synonymous with *paradidōmi*.

35. Wedderburn, 88, ". . . it is God's prerogative to show mercy as God chooses (cf., e.g., 9.15–17) and in fact the divine choice and decision is to show it to all (11:32)."

36. Paul's word in 11:32 is συνέκλεισεν (*synekleisen, imprison*). It is used by Paul only here and in Gal 3:22, 23, where he says, "But the scripture has *imprisoned* all things under the power of sin, so that what was promised through faith in Jesus Christ might be given to those who believe. Now before faith came, we were *imprisoned* and guarded under the law until faith would be revealed." It is thus a statement about God's work through the law. Luke 5:6 uses the word relative to the great catch of fish. Ps 31:8 uses the word to declare, (You) "have not *delivered* me into the hand of the enemy; you have set my feet in a broad place."

inner meaning of Christianity, which defies analysis. The Church hopes. Well, this is the hope of the Church. There is no other hope. Would that the Church might comprehend it! 'Take to heart this great text. By it the whole righteousness of the world and of men is damned: by it the righteousness of God is alone exalted, the righteousness of God which is by faith' (Luther).

Ninth, *the due penalty for their error* likely points to the immoral life itself, not to some secondary penalty such as a physical disease. That is, ". . . the fall into specifically Gentile sins is depicted as a suitable retribution for the guilt of idolatry presented in 22f., 25, and 28a . . ." Contrasted to our usual way of thinking in cause and effect terms, ". . . Paul paradoxically reverses the cause and consequence: Moral perversion is the result of God's wrath, not the reason for it . . ."[37] The reason for God's wrath is idolatry. Paul fits his illustrative comments about sexuality into this argument against idolatry.

As we consider our own context and understanding of texts today we are reminded that, "Interpretation is inevitably a conversation between the reader and the text."[38] We can also say that the conversation is inevitably interpretation: the text's interpretation of us, our understanding of what the text means.[39] There is no reading, or translation, of Scripture without the dynamic of interpretation. The text brings news to us. We bring our awareness and questions to it. So, the Romans passage before us brings certain challenges.

The first challenge is to acknowledge that Paul did not have the same information that we have today. He addressed abusive

37. Thus Käsemann, 44, 47. See also Scroggs, 115–16.

38. Hultgren, "Scriptures," 320.

39. The subject of interpretation brings us to the subject of the authority of Scripture. It is clear that this question of authority is in need of study, reflection, and conversation. The subject of the Bible and homosexuality, and churches' relation to that subject, is highly emotional and deeply conflicted. Disagreements or differences of perspective are often cast in terms of accusation that the authority of Scripture has been abandoned, the traditional faith is being denied, and personal motivations are overly involved. The need for faithful reason and reasoning faith, aiming at clarity, confronts us.

behavior by perpetrators who had power over their victims, but he did not address the question of essential orientation. If anything, this fact makes the text more poignant and pertinent regarding abuse and violence. The texts do *not* allow themselves to be used in condemning persons not guilty of such sins but who have a sexual orientation that is part of their personal nature. In our time, two concepts are firmly fixed in our common life that derive from scientific studies. The first is the concept of sexual orientation; and the second is that one's heterosexual or homosexual orientation is not a matter of choice, but likely a complex matter of nature and nurture.[40]

The second challenge is to acknowledge distinctions that Paul did not: "There are different kinds of homosexuality; there are *homosexualities.*"[41] Thus, when we speak of homosexuals and the homosexual agenda, which homosexuals and what agenda do we mean? There is homosexual activity in prisons or by persons who do it for kicks but who consider themselves heterosexual. Persons who are homosexual by orientation or self-understanding include some who are promiscuous, some who are abstinent, and some who are in committed relationships.

Third, in Romans 1 Paul speaks against the homosexual activity that he knew from his world. This included widespread pederasty and promiscuity among Gentiles. But, "he would not have encountered a person who says: 'I am a Christian. I am homosexual.'"[42] This is at once the newness of our situation and the challenge to understand the biblical text with facts and fairness to the text itself and to the world of our time.

Fourth, at the heart of Reformation theology is the distinction between law and gospel. The distinction must be learned in every generation lest law and gospel, and their respective functions and purpose, be confused.[43] Three comments about law are timely.

One function of law relates to the protection of society, the keeping of civil order, and maintenance of public good. Hence,

40. Hultgren, "Scriptures," 320.

41. Ibid., 321.

42. Ibid., 322.

43. Elert, *Law and Gospel*, is a small but helpful resource.

"specific laws must be altered in light of new conditions, new understanding—precisely for the good order of society. In the light of what we know, it is evident that the first use of the law should extend to the protection of persons who identify themselves as homosexuals."[44] This is the realm of civil rights and equal justice under law, producing safety and civility in and for a nation and society.

A second function of law has to do with identification and accusation of sin. Paul acknowledges this very thing in Rom 3:20 when he says, ". . . through the law comes knowledge of sin." This stark statement of the law's policing and judicial work is enclosed fore and aft by statements of the law's inability to bring about a right relationship with God (*justification*, in the Bible's terminology). Contrary to making things right, the law would hold us accountable for what is wrong (3:19). This is a common theme in the Psalms of the Old Testament, and Paul refers to Psalm 143:2 in Rom 3:20. He levels the playing field on the question of righteousness.

A third comment about law involves what biblical law says about itself. There is an *all or nothing* character to the law: to transgress any particular admonition of the law is to be in violation of all aspects of the whole law. Similarly, to subscribe to a particular aspect of the law is to be obligated to all of the law. We see this in such texts as Deut 27:26; 28:1–2; Leviticus 26. Paul is clear about this in Gal 3:10, as is James 2:10.

Perhaps in North America in particular it is common for church people to think of religion as a matter of choices, even relative to the content or teachings of the religion itself. Many people throughout the church treat the message of the faith as an *ala carte* menu of ideas and doctrines, or a supermarket where one selects from the shelves only those items one chooses to buy. Beliefs are then those notions chosen from the greater whole, selected for what is amenable to one's own life.[45] No little amount of consternation is caused by this approach to the Bible and homosexuality. The approach itself is its own curse. We need a better way.

---

44. Hultgren, "Scriptures," 322. Protection could include the use of legal and ecclesiastical covenants.

45. See Bibby, *Fragmented Gods*.

# 9

## God's Long-term Plan

*Romans 1:16–32 (cont.)*


### GOD GAVE THEM UP

ALTHOUGH PAUL USES THE phrase *God gave them up* three times
in Romans 1, his purpose is not to instill hopelessness, but rather
to point the way of salvation from human sin that God has accomplished for all people. We note three things about these texts.

First, God does not force actions or consequences upon people
but leaves them to the results of actions they have taken and choices
they have made. This is God's judgment, God's wrath, the inevitable
course of God's justice. Second, we note the involvement of hearts,
bodies, passions, and minds. The effects of idolatry invade every
aspect of human existence and all dimensions of the self. They are
the same dimensions with which one is called to love God (Deut
6:5; Matt 22:7; Mark 12:30; Luke 10:27). Third, the illustrations of
the effects of idolatry are secondary to Paul's main purpose and
theological structure. This is borne out by the fact that the illustrations of the effects are interchangeable among the various aspects

and dimensions of human existence. For instance, the illustration of sexual aberration could as easily have gone under the first part—the dishonoring of body.[1] There is a long list of vices associated with the third *God gave them up* (28).[2] This list, too, could have fit just as well in the first or second uses of the phrase. Paul, therefore, is not concerned to attack particular vices so much as to point to the basic human problem (idolatry) and God's solution in Christ.

The use of the verb, *gave up*, with God as the subject of the verb, is not a novelty to Paul nor was it introduced to others by way of Paul's hand. In the Old Testament there are references to the Lord giving up Israel's enemies *into Israel's hands* (Deut 32:30; Josh 11:8; Judg 1:4). The reverse is also true. The Lord gave up Israel *into the hands of its enemies* when the Israelites "did what was evil in the sight of the Lord" (Judg 2:14; 13:1). This giving/handing over was for the sake of Israel's repentance and return to covenant life: "Then the LORD raised up judges, *who delivered them* out of the power of those who plundered them" (Judg 2:16).

Perhaps the most theologically significant use of the word and idea by the church comes from Isa 53:12. Here "the mission and violent death of a servant of the LORD" is told in the last of the four Servant Songs (52:13—53:12; the other three are 42:1-4; 49:1-6; 50:4-11).[3] These passages were applied to Jesus by early Christian tradition that understood him *both* as having been acted upon by betrayal, arrest, and subjection to death by forces aligned against him *and* giving or pouring out of his life by Jesus himself.[4]

1. Scroggs, 113-14, for the aforementioned three points. The verb παρέδωκεν (*paredoken*), *gave up or handed over*, is aorist tense, akin to English past tense, indicating accomplished action.

2. ". . . debased mind, wickedness, evil, covetousness, malice, envy, murder, strife, deceit, craftiness, gossips, slanderers, God-haters, insolent, haughty, boastful, inventors of evil, rebellious toward parents, foolish, faithless, heartless, ruthless, they not only do (such things) but applaud others who practice them." Paul follows so closely the common Jewish idea that the vices of paganism are the result of idolatry that this passage could almost be taken as a summary of the idea and its use. Such lists grouped the vices into sensual and anti-social categories. See Dodd, *Romans*, 27, and Black, 51-2.

3. Blenkinsopp, 1035, 1052-53.

4. Hoad, 254-5. In Isa. 53:12 the verb occurs twice, first in the NRSV as,

The same verb is used in the NT gospels to carry the story of Christ's passion, as he was betrayed, arrested, and delivered up or handed over to crucifixion. All these actions are told with the same verb! We note several examples: the betrayal of Jesus by Judas (Mark 14:10); the handing over of Jesus to Pilate by the Sanhedrin (Mark 15:1); the delivering up by Pilate to the will of the people (Luke 23:25); the handing over to the soldiers for execution (Mark 15:15).[5]

Paul uses a different form of this verb to tell of Christ *giving himself* for us (Gal 1:4; 2:20). This indicates the destiny and purpose of Christ's life and mission: the purpose, *he gave himself for our sins*; the destiny, *according to the will of God*. The self-giving-sacrifice of Christ is indicated by this verb of redemption as it serves Paul's purpose of proclamation. We will return to Paul's purpose statement in Rom 11:32: "For God has imprisoned all in disobedience so that he may be merciful to all." But first we need

---

*poured out (his soul/self)*, and then as, *made intercession (for the transgressors)*. Cullman, 65–9, and Jeremias, 712–17 maintain that the interpretation of the Servant in Isaiah as applied to Jesus goes back to Jesus himself. Manson, 124–27, and Dodd's study of *testimonies*, the use and interpretation of OT passages by NT writers applied to particular themes of the Gospel or Christian theology, in *According To The Scriptures*, 28–60. Dodd, 92–6, 103, 108, 118, 123, 125 points out that the early Christian mission included both preaching of the message as well as discussion, as it struggled to sort out what the message meant. For answers they turned to the Old Testament, and interpreted some of its passages as applying to Jesus. Isaiah 53 was one such text and Jesus was associated with the Suffering Servant who in self-sacrifice suffered and gave himself for the good of the many. Isaiah 53 was thus among the early Christian testimonies that utilized the Old Testament to help followers understand Jesus, his work, and perhaps most of all, his death.

5. Büchsel, "παραδίδωμι," 169–73. *Paradidomi* can be translated as *betray, hand over, arrest, deliver up*. The NT texts that use any form of this verb include: Matt 4:12; 5:25; 10:4, 17, 19, 21; 11:27; 17:22; 18:34; 20:18f; 24:9f; 25:14, 20, 22; 26:2, 15f, 21, 23ff, 45f, 48; 27:2ff, 18, 26; Mark 1:14; 3:19; 4:29; 7:13; 9:31; 10:33; 13:9, 11f; 14:10f, 18, 21, 41f, 44; 15:1, 10, 15; Luke 1:2; 4:6; 9:44; 10:22; 12:58; 18:32; 20:20; 21:12, 16; 22:4, 6, 21f, 48; 23:25; 24:7, 20; John 6:64, 71; 12:4; 13:2, 11, 21; 18:2, 5, 30, 35f; 19:11, 16, 30; 21:20; Acts 3:13; 6:14; 7:42; 8:3; 12:4; 14:26; 15:26, 40; 16:4; 21:11; 22:4; 27:1; 28:17; Rom 1:24, 26, 28; 4:25; 6:17; 8:32; 1 Cor 5:5; 11:2, 23; 13:3; 15:3, 24; 2 Cor 4:11; Gal 2:20; Eph 4:19; 5:2, 25; 1 Tim 1:20; 1 Pet 2:23; 2 Pet 2:4, 21; Jude 1:3.

to look more closely at these three important texts and their uses of *God gave them up* in Romans 1.

## Romans 1:24

The word *therefore* at the beginning of Rom 1:24 indicates a cause and effect construction: "*Therefore* God gave them up in the lusts of their hearts to impurity, to the degrading of their bodies among themselves." *Therefore* follows the catalog of conditions in Rom 1:18–23 that describe the ungodliness, wickedness, and suppression of truth to which Paul has referred in 1:18. Conditions of idolatry are the *cause* of which the *effect* is that God gave up the doers into impurity.

This first occurrence in Romans 1 of the phrase, *God gave them up*, echoes the Old Testament in two ways. First, God could deliver the people of Israel over to their enemies in order ultimately to rescue them. Paul applies that same paradigm to the Gentile world of which he has been speaking. *And it is for the same ultimate purpose of rescue!*[6] Second, speaking of Gentiles Paul says, "God gave them up . . . *to impurity*."[7] But again, the impurity is

6. Käsemann, 46, notes: ". . . for Paul the history of Israel documented in Scripture has exemplary significance for the world . . . Israel's history is relevant for world history . . ." Hence, what has been true of the covenant of God with Israel is now extended to the Gentiles, to cover both Gentile sin and salvation.

7. The word Paul uses, ἀκαθαρσία (*akatharsia/uncleanness, impurity*) in Rom 1:24 occurs often in the Greek translation of the Hebrew Scriptures or Old Testament. That translation, the Septuagint (abbreviated: LXX), was the standard text for Jews like Paul. As a rule it is the text from which the gospel and epistle writers of the New Testament quoted when referring to Scripture. Hays, x–xi, writes of Paul's use of Scripture or what Christians call the Old Testament: "It would be misleading, however, to refer to this Scripture as the Hebrew Bible, because the original Hebrew language of the biblical writings was not a concern of Paul. His citations characteristically follow the Septuagint (LXX), a Greek translation of the Hebrew Bible dating from the second or third century B.C.E., which was in common use in Hellenistic synagogues during Paul's lifetime." Paul is not quoting here in 1:24 but he is using a word that was common in the vocabulary of his religious history. The OT references included in this section of our study for the tracing of the word *uncleanness*,

not the final stage, purpose, or destination of divine action. The purpose, rather, is salvation.

The concept of *impurity* was familiar to Paul from the history of his own Jewish people. We note some examples of the use and development of the concept as it occurs in the Law, the Prophets, Jesus, the Acts of the Apostles, and Paul.

*The law* of the Old Testament speaks often and clearly about *impurity* or *uncleanness*, using the same word that occurs here in Rom 1:24.[8] *Uncleanness* refers to the condition of a thing that is to be avoided or shunned, a person who is rendered unfit for the presence of God or a holy place, or an item that has been polluted by the uncleanness of the people. Leviticus 15, for example, tells of the temporary uncleanness of a man following sexual discharge and of a woman during her time of menstruation. Uncleanness in this sense is distinct from sins and transgressions (see Lev 16:16).

*Uncleanness* can also refer to inappropriate sexual relationships, such as a man's taking of his brother's wife (Lev 20:21), or to things that are declared unclean, such as certain forbidden animals (Lev 20:25). Leviticus 11 especially distinguishes between clean and unclean foods.[9]

*Uncleanness* is contrary to holiness or separateness: "You shall be holy to me; for I the LORD am holy, and I have separated you from the other peoples to be mine." (Lev 20:26). Transgression requires religious cleansing so that a person can be restored to normal life in the covenant community and to worship.[10] In the Priestly Code of Leviticus 1–16, *tolerable uncleanness* requires religious cleansing for the sake of one's restoration to covenant relationship and worship. Uncleanness, or impurity, is redeemed by sacrifice, times of separation, acts of obedience, or priestly rituals. Leviticus also refers to *intolerable uncleanness* that cannot be overcome by

---

*impurity*, follow the LXX.

8. Hebrew, טֻמְאָה (ṭəmēʾāʰ): Lev 5:3; 7:20, 21; 15:3, 25, 26, 30, 31; 18:19; 19:23; 20:21, 25; 22:3, 4, 5; Num 19:13.

9. Schwartz, 229, ". . . these laws provide the biblical basis for the laws of 'kashrut' practiced to this day."

10. D. Wright, "Leviticus," 156.

temporary separation, ritual washing, or priestly function. Such impurities relate to transgression of forbidden sexual relationships, the result of which is that the transgressors would be *cut off from their people* (18:29) and *the land will vomit you out for defiling it* (18:28). The prohibitions would protect Israel from failure to be distinct from their predecessors in the land, which would mean loss of land or loss of place in the community.[11]

*Prophets* spoke of ethical uncleanness, meaning Israel's apostasy, breaking covenant, idolatry and going after other gods (Hos 2:10). Idolatry defiled the land (Ezek 36:17). Such messages of doom were often commentaries on the loss of land and the exile of its people.[12] This ethical aspect relates to the question of values: "The prophets rate ethical purity far above that which is purely cultic. Hence the prophets prepare the way for the religion of Jesus."[13]

*Jesus* carried on the prophets' ethical heritage when he exclaimed woe against the scribes and Pharisees for inward uncleanness (Matt 23:27). He compared them to whitewashed tombs, beautiful on the outside but inside full of all kinds of *uncleanness*, appearing righteous on the outside, but inside full of hypocrisy and lawlessness. It is notable that the thing against which Jesus spoke in the scribes and Pharisees was how they would *lock people out of the kingdom of heaven* (Matt 23:13) and yet they *neglected the weightier matters of the law: justice and mercy and faith* (Matt 23:23).

*Acts* 10:28 relays Peter's recognition of the same weighty matters of justice, mercy, and faith. He reflected the breadth of Jesus' mission as it applied to life in community for persons and peoples. No one is common or *unclean*.[14] No person is beyond grace, faith, and entry into the faith community. This signals the *scandal* of

11. Ibid., 156.

12. See Ezek 4:14; 7:20; 9:9; 22:10,15; 24:11; 36:17, 25, 29; 39:24; Hos 2:12; Mic 2:10; Nah 3:6; Jer 19:13; 39:34.

13. Hauck, "καθαρός, καθαρίζω, κτλ.," 417.

14. The gospels and Acts use a related term, *akathartos* (impure, unclean), frequently: Matt 10:1; 12:43; Mark 1:23, 26, 27; 3:11, 30; 5:2, 8, 13; 6:7; 7:25; 9:25; Luke 4:33, 36; 6:18; 8:29; 9:42; 11:24; Acts 5:16; 8:7, 10, 14, 28; 11:8. It is often related to idolatry, can be used of the evil/unclean spirits, indicates *without relationship to God* and shows a thing not purged. See Haenchen, 350.

the gospel and how it would shake the Christian community as it struggled with the relationship of Jew and Gentile to one another and to God. If inclusion in the community of Christ truly is by faith alone, then the old barriers and distinctions of law are surpassed. In Christ there is neither Jew nor Greek.[15]

*Paul* uses the word *akatharsia* in Rom 6:19 to speak of the Romans' former slavery to *impurity* and to iniquity (lawlessness). In 2 Cor 12:21 and Gal 5:19 he uses it in connection with sexual immorality (*porneia*, from which we get the word *pornography*). His anxiety about the Corinthians is that some will not have repented of the things they have practiced. In Galatians 5 Paul lists a catalog of works of the flesh that are contrary to the Spirit. Among the list is *impurity*.[16] Paul's use of *God gave them up* in 1:24 shows the effect of the cause (idolatry) explained in 1:18–23. So also 1:25 reaffirms the construction by stating again the cause behind consignment to impurity: worship of the creature rather than the Creator. It is in fact this problem—unbelief, outsiders, and enemies of truth—that Paul deals with throughout the epistle. He addresses the cause, the core problem, with the truth of his gospel.

## Romans 1:26–27

This is the second occurrence in the trilogy of phrases (*God gave them up*). *Degrading passions*, consists of an adjective (degrading) and a noun (passions). But in the Greek text the phrase is two nouns, *pathē*, referring to passive emotions or desires, and *atimia*, referring to dishonor or disgrace. The first noun, *pathē*, suggests passions that befall a person, which the person endures or suffers. It is a word always used in a negative or bad sense, sometimes of violent emotions.[17] Thus, in 1 Thes 4:5 Paul

---

15. On *faith alone* for relationships in the Christ community, see Dahl, "Justification," 95–120. Munck, 228–234, is also helpful.

16. For other Pauline texts see Eph 4:19; 5:3; Col 3:5; 1 Thes 2:3; 4:7. For the related term, *akathartos*, in Paul see 1 Cor 7:14; 2 Cor 6:17; Eph 5:5.

17. Abbott-Smith, 332–33, for πάθη (*pathē*).

encourages believers each to control his or her own body in holiness and honor, and *not with lustful passion.*

The second noun, *atimia, (dishonor* or *disgrace)* is a stronger word. [18] It can refer to a man's wearing long hair (1 Cor 11:14), Paul's own experience of ill-treatment for the sake of his ministry (2 Cor 6:8), and the sowing in dishonor (death and burial) of the fleshly body that awaits new life and glory in resurrection (1 Cor 15:43). But he doesn't stop there. Paul says, *not with lustful passion, like the Gentiles who do not know God.* That is, Paul here makes a rather standard Jewish judgment of associating the Gentiles with such behavior of lustful passion attributed to their not knowing God. [19] This is similar to Paul's reference to *Gentile sinners* in Gal 2:15, and Rom 1:18–32, wherein *they* and *them* of whom Paul speaks are the citizens of the pagan, Gentile world. [20]

Paul began v. 26 with the phrase, *For this reason.* We may ask, for *what* reason? He has previously stated the reasons that amount to idolatry: ungodliness, wickedness, suppression of the truth, v. 18; not honoring or thanking God, v. 21; exchanging the immortal God for mortal images, v. 23; exchanging the truth about God for a lie, v. 25; worshipping the creature rather than the Creator, v. 25.

The result is that God gave them up to impurity (24) and to degrading passions (26a), resulting in the exchange of the natural for the unnatural (26b). The impurity and the degrading passions

---

18. Ibid., 67, for ἀτιμία (*atimia*).

19. Smith, 343, says that 1 Thes 4:5 is, "a typical slur against Gentiles (Ps 79:6; Jer 10.25)."

20. Elliot, 46, points out that when Paul speaks of an inidvidual he refers to the person as Jew, Greek, or another national, ethnic, or regional identity characterization. It may be more accurate socially and theologically to speak of *the nations* rather than *the Gentiles. The nations* is indeed what *ta ethnē* means. Elliot says of the term *Gentiles,* "Although many New Testament scholars follow the NRSV in using the translation (with a capital 'G', suggesting a distinct ethnic identity equivalent but opposite to Jews), the notion that non–Judeans in the Roman congregations would have thought of themselves as Gentiles is unsustainable." He cites Munck, who said that Paul *thinks in nations,* and Georgi, who said that Paul saw himself as the apostle *to the peoples of this earth at large.* Paul proclaimed the universality of God's rule, and that rule was implemented through the Messiah.

are not the reason for which God gave them up. The reason for which God gave them up is their idolatry. The impurity and the degrading passions are the controlling forces into which the persons were given up. So the impurity and the degrading passions are the effect, the cause of which is the idolatry characteristic of the pagan/Gentile world about which Paul is writing.[21]

Paul does not specify what *natural* and *unnatural* mean in Rom 1:26–7, but he applies the terms to both men and women in ways that indicate he is referring to sexual intercourse.[22] He does this by stating in v. 26 that women have exchanged their natural *use* or *function* (*chrēsin*, here in the sexual sense) for what is *para physin*, against or beyond nature.[23] Then in v. 27, Paul says implicitly that the same thing is true of males: *and in the same way also the men.*

The translation, *unnatural*, represents two words in the Greek text that could mean, *against nature.*[24] *Nature* and the *natural* would have been understood, whether in Jewish or Gentile, religious or secular settings, to include *a fundamental cultural rule* representing the *conventional. Unnatural* then indicates something that is *seriously unconventional.* This would represent one line of

21. Käsemann, 47, recognizes Paul's paradoxical reversal of usual cause and effect consequences: "Moral perversion is the result of God's wrath, not the reason for it . . . it brings about the surrender of existence to determination by the world, which will later be called σάρξ (*sic: sarx/flesh*). This means its abandonment to chaos." *Then* God saves.

22. See Hultgren, *Romans*, 96–98 for a discussion of the range of possibilities for the meaning of *natural-unnatural*, whether (1) customary, (2) natural order, or (3) divinely created order.

23. Abbott–Smith, 484; BDAG, 894. Key here is the exchange as a rational, deliberate decision or choice.

24. Käsemann, 48, says that the words, παρὰ φύσιν (*para physin*) in v. 26, "demonstrate degeneration: People refuse to be bound by the order immanent in the world and in humanity." See Köster, 273.

thought shared by Paul with the times in which he lived.[25] What is *unnatural* or *against nature* deviates from the ordinary.[26]

But the terminology of *natural* and *unnatural* can also take us beyond the sense of conventional and unconventional. Indeed, the prepositional phrase, *para physin* in v. 26, often translated as *against nature*, can also signify *beyond nature*. If it were taken to mean *against* then the sense would be *contrary to nature*. That is, the only kind of sexual relationship that is in keeping with nature is that between a male and a female. If the phrase were taken to mean *beyond nature*, then it would mean that the women and men who are represented by this text have exceeded the usual limits that have been established by nature. They will have exceeded what is normal and the excess would indicate lustful behavior due to having been *consumed with passion.*[27] It could also indicate that the woman has abandoned the usually passive female sexual role and taken a more active or assertive part in the sexual relationship. The active or assertive role in sexual intercourse had been reserved for men, and for women to take on the normally male gender role as the assertive partner (with either male or female) would thus go *beyond nature*, that is, beyond the usual limits and boundaries of what tradition considered natural. It would also be a situation shaming to the husband. Nissinen identifies the problem as unnatural *heterosexual* activity.[28]

25. Fitzmyer, *Romans*, 286, referrences the *Letter of Aristeas* that suggests, ". . . such unnatural sexual practices were characteristic of 'most of the rest of mankind' or of 'whole countries and cities', but not of the Jewish people: 'we have been set apart from these things.'" See Scroggs, 92, who further reports this thought, "Among the sins of the Gentiles are male homosexuality and incest." Paul's thought links idolatry and homosexual activity. See Scroggs, 60, for the idea that *para physin* as used by Paul in Rom 1:26–27 refers to pederasty and ". . . is the most common stereotype of Greco-Roman attitudes."

26. Nissinen, 105. The Greeks accepted pederasty as common and natural. Jews did not and Paul here "freely reproduces the teaching of the Hellenistic Jewish synagogue." See Köster, 271–275.

27. Hultgren, *Romans*, 97–99, has helpful discussion of these points. He quotes (98 n. 58) Pelagius, "Lust, once unbridled, knows no limit."

28. See Nissinen, 107–8; Hultgren, *Romans*, 99, especially n. 65.

Overall, it seems that Paul and the other biblical authors did not think of two types of persons, heterosexual and homosexual. They seem to have thought singularly of human persons and their sexuality, some of whom Paul knows have abandoned what they had practiced previously, and exchanged their natural sexual lives for something else. Excessive passion, uncontrolled lust, and exploitation of others became the consequences, all the result of idolatry. This characterizes the persons who have not honored God.[29] Given Paul's argument about righteousness and wrath these verses cannot be taken as intending to exclude but rather finally include *all (who) have sinned* (3:23) so that they may be among *all who believe* (3:22).

Paul speaks of *nature/physis* in other Romans texts and in somewhat different ways, but again in relation to boundaries. In 2:14 he refers to Gentiles who *instinctively*, or *naturally*, do what the law requires despite not having the law. This natural or instinctive law obedience shows that for such law–abiding Gentiles the law is written on their hearts, their consciences bear witness to it, and in the judgment they will be accused or excused by it. In 2:27 Paul refers to those who *by nature/physically* are uncircumcised. Here again, he speaks of Gentiles, and we recognize how much he has their situation at heart. In 2:25–9 Paul renders a kind of commentary on the supposition that the whole law is involved in any of its single aspects or regulations: to transgress one regulation is to transgress the whole, and to commit to one aspect is to engage the entire law. As a result, there is no singling out of solitary legal references to condemn or to excuse. This precept of all or nothing, with respect to law, is missed in much current discussion that often flows from treating Scripture as a dry goods catalog where only one's preference, selection, and choice are decisive.

Furthermore, Paul would have us understand that being a Jew has nothing to do with blood and soil, birth and background.

29. Elliot, 78: "It is now well established that the classical world did not conceive of what we today call homosexual orientation, a natural erotic preference for others of the same gender, as distinct from heterosexual orientation. Paul's contemporaries perceived a single reality, sexul desire, which could attach to people of either gender. How much less likely is it that Paul would feel constrained to offer an explanation of homosexual desire!"

Rather, it is "a matter of the heart—it is spiritual and not literal" (v. 29). Nationhood, race, and ethnicity do not enter into the question of God's call and human response. The call is by grace, the response is by faith, and the addition of any other condition remains an oft-repeated human scheme against which present day faith also needs steadfastly to stand. Romans 3 summarizes Paul's message: all, both Jews and Greeks, are under the power of sin (3:9b); for all the knowledge of sin comes through the law, and this, not the bringing of justification, is the law's function (3:20); now for all who believe, the righteousness of God has been disclosed apart from the law, through faith in Jesus Christ (3:21).

The God who transcends boundaries has established a new efficacy for salvation, namely justification (righteousness) *by his grace as a gift, through the redemption that is in Christ Jesus* (3:24). The law is not dead, has not disappeared, and is not bad. It just does not save, does not inspire faith, and cannot make alive or establish a right relation to God.[30] Romans 11:21 and 24 are helpfully instructive texts that explicitly describe how God's redemptive activity has overcome the natural human limitations of those who were initially outside the covenant of election and grace. Paul refers to Israel as the *natural* branches of the olive tree (16, 17, 19, 21) and the Gentiles as the wild olive shoot (17) that has been grafted into the tree so as to give Gentiles, the grafted branches, a share in the root. The point of this section comes in v. 24 as Paul addresses Gentile believers: "For if you have been cut from what is *by nature* a wild olive tree and grafted, *contrary to nature*, into a cultivated olive tree, how much more will these *natural* branches be grafted back into their own olive tree."

Here we meet Paul's sense of the universal diversity of the church, the body of Christ. His point is that not only are Gentiles, the outsiders from Israel's point of view, now brought by faith into

---

30. Paul understands that he has died to the old aeon so that he may live in God's new order: he has died in relation to the law, so to live in relation to God (Rom 7:4; Gal 2:19). For a serious consideration of Paul and the law by a little-known Minnesota theologian see Gary Gilthvedt, "Dying Through the Law to the Law' (Gal 2:19)" at: www.ntgateway.com/paul-the-apostle/galatians/galatiansbooks-and-articles.

the church, but the same church must also include Israel itself. The church is incomplete until all are there, both Jew and Gentile, following God's redemptive breaking of *natural* boundaries and overcoming *unnatural* characteristics. All believers in Christ have been grafted into the same life–giving root.

We note that, in making his case, Paul does not cite the creation narratives from Genesis 1–3, nor does he refer to Gentile shamelessness as a consequence of Adam's sin. What is *natural* is not equated with a particular theology of creation based in Genesis material. He can speak of Gentiles' natural or instinctive obedience in 2:14, when Gentiles do by nature what the law requires.[31] Paul can also equate natural order with divine order, and the disordering of natural order, as illustrated by *unnatural* sexual practices, is a logical consequence of idolatry. Idolatry is the problem Paul wants to emphasize so as to establish the need for God's gift of grace in Christ for all people.

## Romans 1:28

Paul recapitulates in Rom 1:28 what he has laid out in the preceding ten verses. But now he begins with the cause or reason for God's decision: *they did not see fit to acknowledge God.* As a consequence God gave them up to a debased mind and to things that should not be done. This is not the sole reference to *mind* in Paul's writings. The *mind* has a powerfully evangelical place in Paul's message.[32]

---

31. Fitzmyer, *Romans*, 309, indicates that the absence of the definite article with *ethnē* (nations, Gentiles) points to *some* Gentiles (rather than all) who by nature do *some* of the things of the law (but not all of it). Paul does not argue for a natural law or natural ability to fulfill the whole law, but rather for a natural ability on the part of some people to do some of the things that the law requires, that is, "by the regular, natural order of things" some Gentiles frame rules of conduct for themselves. The NRSV translates regarding Gentiles who "do instinctively what the law requires." Fitzmyer, 310, also argues that Paul here refers to Gentiles as such, not specifically to Gentile Christians. See Käsemann, *Romans*, 63.

32. The noun is *nous*: mind, thought, reason, attitude, intention, purpose, understanding, discernment. The deutero-Pauline epistles speak of the *mind* in Eph 4:17, 23; Col 2:18; 2 Thes 2:2; 1 Tim 6:5; 2 Tim 2:8; Titus 1:15.

In Romans the mind is the field of conflict between service to God and slavery to sin (7:23, 25); it is the seat of God's unknowable counsel (11:34); it is the center of transformation for the believer (12:2); it is the place of discernment and conviction (14:5).

In 1 Corinthians the mind is the home of agreement, overcoming of divisions, and union of purpose (1:10); it is the believers' gift of Christ's own mind (2:16); it is the vehicle of prayer (14:14, 15, 19).

In Philippians the mind is kept in Christ by God's peace (4:7). Such soaring assertions about the mind that is captured and propelled for God's service stand in stark contrast to the debased mind to which God has given up those who have not acknowledged God as God.

The *mind of Christ* is specifically mentioned in Rom 11:34 and 1 Cor 2:16. Similarly, Paul speaks in Phil 2:5 of reflecting or sharing the mind of Christ himself. To express this, Paul uses a verb that means *to think the thoughts of (i.e. someone else), to have one's mind controlled by.*[33] Paul thus encourages Christian ethics: conforming to the mind of Christ, and knowing Christ's mind through the means of Christ's message and mission.

That God *gave them up to a debased mind* is not an end in itself but a means to an end. The end is redemption. It is credible to assert that the divine act of *giving up* (or *giving over*) is for the sake of final inclusion and not for irreversible exclusion, for ultimate transformation and not for excommunication, for redemption and not for condemnation.[34]

For example, Rom 4:25 tells of Jesus' death and resurrection for our sakes: "(He) was *handed over* to death for our trespasses

---

33. The verb, φρονέω, (*phroneo*), occurs also in Rom 8:5; 11:20; 12:3, 16; 14:6; 15:5; 1 Cor 13:11; 2 Cor 13:11; Gal 5:10; Phil 1:7; 2:2, 5; 3:15, 19; 4:2, 10.

34. See Matt 18:15–17, often regarded as a church guide for discipline. Mary Gilthvedt, *If A Member Sins Against You*, 65–7, ably argues that when the process of discipline is carried out by those who "live and breathe a spirit of forgiveness" and "who know that they themselves are the unworthy recipients of God's constant mercy and forgiveness" (66) then a transgressor's eventual restoration is better served. It is in the character of God to restore the lost and fallen.

No Condemnation!

and was raised for our justification."³⁵ The traditions of Jesus' betrayal, arrest, and being handed over consistently use *gave up/over*, the verb of the passion, as Paul does also here in 4:25, to tell of God's redemptive purpose carried out in Jesus' life, death, and resurrection. This thread is particularly evident in Mark (9:31; 10:33; 14:10–11, 21; 15:1, 15).

The source of this line of thought may have its roots in Isaiah 53:12, *"Therefore I will allot him a portion with the great, and he shall divide the spoil with the strong; because he poured out himself to death, and was numbered with the transgressors; yet he bore the sin of many, and made intercession for the transgressors."*³⁶

First Corinthians 5:5 could be considered an extreme example of *handing over, delivering* or *giving up*, in this case of a man who is cohabiting with his (apparently) widowed step–mother. The verb used here is the same as the threefold use of *giving up* in Rom 1:24–8, although in a different form. Paul instructs the Corinthian assembly, "You are to *hand* this man *over* to Satan for the destruction of the flesh, *so that* his spirit may be saved in the day of the Lord."³⁷ Salvation or restoration is the ultimate goal. Condemnation is not the end–game.

35. That is, "on account of our trespasses, for the sake of our justification." The word *justification* (δικαίωσις/*dikaiosis*) is formed on the same root as the word for righteousness. Here it may be helpful to translate as *amnesty.* See Manson, 29–81, especially 54; acquittal is declaring one not guilty who is found to be not guilty, whereas amnesty is pardoning one who has in fact committed an offense. Paul's point throughout this section of Romans is that all are included in Christ's redemptive work because all are in need of Christ's redemptive work. See also Ziesler on *Righteousness in Paul.*

36. The LXX uses our verb, παρεδόθη (*paredothē*/poured out, gave himself) twice in Isa. 53:12. Paul uses the same passive in Rom 4:25, showing the action *upon* Christ *on account of our trespasses* just as the soul/life of the Servant of Isaiah 53 *was delivered* to death and who *was delivered* because or on account of the iniquities of the transgressors. This part of the fourth Servant Song in Isaiah was rendered by early Christians as a description of Christ and his atoning death. See Hoad, "References to Isaiah 53." Rom 8:32 is similar in thought but adds that this *giving up* was *for us all* (ὑπὲρ ἡμῶν/*hyper hemon*). The *our* in 4:25 points to this inclusiveness.

37. The word *flesh* (σαρκός/*sarkos*) can refer to generations of ancestry, to the physical body, or to the power of sin. Here, without contextual emphasis

First Corinthians 13:3, part of the great hymn to love, indicates the unprofitable result even if *I hand over my body* (for martyrdom), but which act, absent love, would be to no avail.[38] Self-absorption is precluded.

Second Corinthians 4:11 mirrors Paul's reflection of mortal existence, *afflicted, crushed, perplexed, persecuted, clay jars,* as vessels for God's extraordinary power. And then he drives home his point: "For while we live, we are always being *given up* to death for Jesus' sake, so that the life of Jesus may be made visible in our mortal flesh."[39] Here the lifelong deathward movement of human mortality, to which we are *given up,* is for the greater good of manifesting the life of Jesus in his messengers' transitory existence. The life of the community is called to reflect the character of God's work in Jesus.[40]

The three texts in Rom 1:24, 26, 28, with the three uses of *God gave them up,* are analogies to the aforementioned ways in which Paul uses *giving up* language to signal God's power, victory, and redemption through Christ. This line of thought is consistent with Paul's pervasive argument in Romans 1–3, that God's saving work is meant for *all* people:

---

on either of the former, it refers to the sinful behavior of the man in question. See Jewett, 96, 453.

38. KJV and ASV translate v. 3b, "give my body to be *burned*," (*kauthēsomai*); NRSV has, "hand over my body so that I may *boast*," (*kauchēsomai*). The latter is less credible than the former: (1) the majority of manuscripts have "burn," and (2) "an act performed in order to glory is already by definition an act without love." See Barrett, 302.

39. In 2 Cor 4:10-11 Paul twice uses the phrase, *the life of Jesus,* the only times throughout his writings. The scarcity of such references reflects Paul having had no contact with the earthly Jesus. Certainly the phrase here would point to Jesus' word and teaching, in harmony with his messengers' gospel (v. 3), proclamation (v. 5), and treasure (v. 7). It is this (message of) the death of Jesus (v. 10) and as well a share in Jesus' suffering and dying, i.e. the cross, that is carried in the messengers' body.

40. The participle, *carrying,* in v. 10 is plural, while the *body* in which carrying happens is singular. Does this point to the community/body as the vehicle of witness, even though the NRSV translates into the plural (bodies) what is singular in Greek?

"For I am not ashamed of the gospel; it is the power of God for salvation *to everyone* who has faith, to the Jew first and also to the Greek" (1:16).

"The righteousness of God has been disclosed . . . through faith in Jesus Christ *for all* who believe" (3:21–2).

"Is God the God of Jews only? Is he not the God of Gentiles also? Yes, *of Gentiles also*, since God is one; and he will justify the circumcised on the ground of faith and the uncircumcised through that same faith" (3:29–30).[41]

Paul repeatedly affirms that to be included in the salvation that God has established in Christ is not an outcome anchored in human spiritual or moral disposition. It rests only on the exchange Christ wrought when he took the human predicament upon himself and in return gave his place in relation to the Father to any and all who would believe. Few places in the Pauline collection speak of this exchange as eloquently as does the Christ–hymn in Phil 2:6–11.[42]

> Let the same mind be in you that was in Christ Jesus, who, though he was in the form of God, did not regard equality with God as something to be exploited, but emptied himself, taking the form of a slave, being born in human likeness. And being found in human form, he humbled himself and became obedient to the point of death—even death on a cross. Therefore God also highly exalted him and gave him the name that is above every name, so that at the name of Jesus every knee should bend, in heaven and on earth and under the earth, and every tongue should confess that Jesus Christ is Lord, to the glory of God the Father.

41. *Circumcised* and *uncircumcised* are common references to Jews and Gentiles respectively. See Gal 2:9. The institution of circumcision as a *sign of the covenant* is in Gen 17:9–14. Carr, 34, calls it "a mark of membership in the covenant community." Brueggemann, *Genesis*, 154, calls it "the sign and seal of trust in the promise and entrance into the covenant" and compares the intention of circumcision to that of baptism (p. 156). See Hyatt.

42. Hooker, "Interchange," 349–361. Christ takes our sin, we receive his grace. He gives us the place he lays aside.

This interchange in Christ involved his becoming what we are, in order that we might become what he is. It was caused by humanity's exchange of its true status and image for an idol and a false identity. But humanity, indeed the whole creation, has been forever effected by God's response, the sending of Christ.

# 10

## Common Ground

WE RETURN TO PAUL'S purpose statement in Rom 11:32: "For God has imprisoned all in disobedience so that he may be merciful to all." In Romans 11 Paul is speaking specifically *about* his own people Israel. But in 11:13 he speaks directly *to* Gentiles. Israel's stumbling (12) benefits the world, Israel's defeat benefits Gentiles, and Israel's rejection has issued in reconciliation for the *kosmos* (15): God's ultimate purpose is to bring all people into grace.

The relation of stumbling and sluggishness on Israel's part and salvation and reconciliation for Gentiles, aimed at Israel's final full inclusion, is akin to the paradigm that we have seen in Judges 2 and 13. There we find the disciplining of Israel for the sake of its repentance and return to covenant faithfulness. The paradigm of discipline and return prevails also in the Priestly Code of Leviticus 1–16, in the setting aside of persons who are unclean until they may return to covenant community life.

The passages about *God gave them up* in Rom 1:24, 26, 28 state a truth that is not an end in itself, but a means to an end. The real end or goal of the *giving up* is clearly stated at the end of Paul's introductory argument in Romans 3:21–2: "But now, apart from law, the righteousness of God has been disclosed . . . the righteousness of

God through faith in Jesus Christ for *all* who believe." He says more in 3:22–4: "For there is no distinction, since *all* have sinned and fall short of the glory of God; *they* are now justified by his grace as a gift, through the redemption that is in Christ Jesus . . ."

In Romans 1 Paul has spoken about practices that, from a Jewish perspective, mark Gentiles as outsiders to the covenant people. But his purpose is not to exclude Gentiles from grace. The texts cited show with their reference to *everyone*, *all* and *Gentiles*, that salvation is open to everyone, on one and the same basis and through one and the same agency: *faith in Christ* (3:30). Faith is *the* ground of inclusion, the agent of amnesty, and the substance of community. In Christ condemnation is cancelled! The gospel of *in Christ, faith alone, no condemnation* is for the whole human family.[1]

The concept of *in Christ* may be the central feature of Paul's thought and literary corpus.[2] It points the church today in the direction it can faithfully and evangelically walk with respect to all persons, including homosexuals. The need of homosexual persons is the need of every person. That need is not curse, but blessing; not rejection, but invitation; not nihilism, but faith; not isolation, but community in Christ, wherein there is no condemnation. Our understanding of homosexuality, as well as the biblical texts that relate to it, will remain a work in progress. At bottom are the age-old questions of who may belong to the kingdom, and how, and in what ways can and may we live in the community of Christ.

The Bible will not always mean what we have thought it to mean in our respective pasts. Such is the Bible's depth and breadth. To search it is arduous work. For the fact is, we are not much

1. BDAG, 412, suggests that κατάκριμα (*katakrima*) should not be translated as condemnation, but as punishment (i.e. consequence of a sentence of judgment), hence, *doom: there is no doom for those who are in Christ Jesus.*

2. Stewart, *A Man in Christ*, vii; Mackay, *God's Order*, 96–121. The list of ἐν Χριστῷ (*en Christo/in Christ*) passages in Pauline material is extensive: Rom 3:24; 6:11, 23; 8:1f, 39; 9:1; 12:5; 14:18; 15:17; 16:3, 7, 9f; 1 Cor 1:2, 4, 30; 3:1; 4:10, 15, 17; 15:18f, 22, 31; 16:24; 2 Cor 2:14, 17; 3:14; 5:17, 19; 12:2, 19; Gal 1:22; 2:4, 17; 3:14, 26, 28; 5:6; Eph 1:1, 3, 10, 12, 20; 2:6f, 10, 13; 3:6, 11, 21; 4:32; 5:24; 6:5; Phil 1:1, 13, 26; 2:1, 5; 3:3, 14; 4:7, 19, 21; Col. 1:2, 4, 28; 2:20; 3:1, 3; 1 Thes 1:1; 2:14; 4:16; 5:18; 2 Thes 1:1; 3:12; 1 Tim 1:14; 3:13; 2 Tim 1:1, 9, 13; 2:1, 10; 3:12, 15; Phlm 1:8, 20, 23.

accustomed to hard wrestling with difficult texts, cognizance of literary conversations and contexts, delineating the distinction between law and gospel, weighing the concerns of the biblical author against the concerns of our own time, and allowing for strenuous growth amidst challenges to our accustomed ways of thinking.

But the challenges elevate the necessity and burnish the promised outcome of renewal for those who are in Christ. If the anxieties and animosities of our time increase the risk of evangelical faith, they also heighten the utility of the church's vocation to live in the assurance that, *"God was in Christ, reconciling the world to himself . . . and giving to us the ministry of reconciliation."* The challenge for us now, dear reader, is to understand human sexuality as an integral component of human existence that awaits such evangelical response.

# Bibliography

Abba, Raymond. "Priests and Levites." In *IDB* 3:876–89.

Abbott-Smith, G. *A Manual Greek Lexicon of the New Testament*. Edinburgh: T. & T. Clark, 1960.

Achtemeier, E. R. "Righteousness in the OT." In *IDB* 4:80–85.

Akenson, Donald. *Saint Saul*. New York: Oxford, 2000.

Amit, Yairah. "Judges." In *JSB* 508–57.

Anderson, Bernhard W. *Understanding The Old Testament*. Englewood Cliffs: Prentice-Hall, 1986.

Baab, O. J. "Concubine." In *IDB* 1:666.

Barrett, C. K. *The First Epistle to the Corinthians*. New York: Harper & Row, 1968.

Barth, Karl. *The Epistle To The Romans*. Translatd by Edwyn Hoskyn. London: Oxford, 1963.

Bassler, Jouette M. "1 Timothy." In *HCSB* 2229–2237.

Bauckham, Richard. "Jude." In *HCSB* 2304–2305.

————. *Jude, 2 Peter* Waco: Word, 1983.

————. *Jude and the Relatives of Jesus in the Early Church*. Edinburgh: T&T Clark, 1990.

Bauer, Walter. *A Greek-English Lexicon of the New Testament and Other Early Christian Literature*. Translated and adapted by W. F. Arndt and F. W. Gingrich. Second edition. Revised and augmented by F. W. Danker and F. W. Gingrich. Chicago: University of Chicago, 1979.

Bibby, Reginald. *Fragmented Gods*. Toronto: Irwin, 1987.

Black, Matthew. *Romans*. Grand Rapids: Eerdmans, 1981.

Blenkinsopp, Joseph. "Isaiah." In *NOAB* 974–1072.

Boling, Robert. "Judges." In *HCSB* 367–407.

————. *Judges*. The Anchor Bible, 6A. New York: Doubleday, 1975.

Bornkamm, Günther. *Jesus Of Nazareth*. Translated by Irene and Fraser McLuskey with James Robinson. New York: Harper, 1960.

Boyarin, Daniel. "Are There Any Jews in the 'History of Sexuality'?" In *Journal of the History of Sexuality* 5.3 (1995): 333–55.

# Bibliography

Braun, Herbert. "πλανάω, πλάνη, κτλ," in *TDNT* VI:228–53.

Brosend, William. "The Letter of Jude: A Rhetoric Of Excess Or An Excess Of Rhetoric?" *Interpretation* 60 (2006) 292–305.

Bultmann, Rudolf. *The Second Letter to the Corinthians.* Translated by Roy Harrisville. Minneapolis: Augsburg, 1985.

————. *Theology Of The New Testament.* Translated by Kendrick Grobel. New York: Scribner's Sons, 1951.

Brueggemann, Walter. *Genesis.* Interpretation: A Bible Commentary for Teaching and Preaching. Atlanta: John Knox, 1982.

————. *The Land.* Philadelphia: Fortress, 1977.

————. *Theology Of The Old Testament.* Minneapolis: Fortress, 1997.

Büchsel, Friedrich and Johannes Herrmann. "ἱλαστήριον, ἵλεως, κτλ.," in *TDNT* III:300–323.

Büchsel, Friedrich. "ἀλλάσσω, μεταλλάσσω, κτλ." In *TDNT* I:251–59.

————. "δίδωμι, παραδίδωμι, κτλ." In *TDNT* II:169–73.

Carr, David. "Genesis." In *NOAB* 9–81.

Conzelmann, Hans. *1 Corinthians.* Translated by James W. Leitch. Philadelphia: Fortress, 1975.

Cullman, Oscar. *Peter.* Translated by Floyd Filson. Philadelphia: Westminster, 1953.

Dahl, Nils. "Contradictions in Scripture." In *Studies In Paul,* 159–77. Minneapolis: Augsburg, 1977.

————. "The Doctrine of Justification: Its Social Function and Implications." In *Studies in Paul,* 95–120.

Dodd, C. H. *According To The Scriptures.* London: Nisbet, 1952.

————. *The Epistle Of Paul To The Romans.* London: Hodder and Stoughton, 1947.

Douglas, Mary. "Justice As The Cornerstone." *Interpretation* 53 (1999) 341–50.

————. *Leviticus as Literature.* Oxford: Oxford, 1999.

————. *Purity and Danger.* London: Routledge, 1966.

Dover, Kenneth. *Greek Homosexuality.* Cambridge: Harvard, 1978.

Dunn, James D. G. "1 Timothy." *NIB* XI:774–831.

Elert, Werner. *Law and Gospel.* Translated by Edward Schroeder. Philadelphia: Fortress, 1967.

Elliott, Neil. *The Arrogance of Nations.* Minneapolis: Fortress, 2010.

Fitzmyer, Joseph. *First Corinthians.* New Haven: Yale, 2008.

————. *Romans.* The Anchor Bible. New Haven: Yale, 2008.

Forsyth, P. T. *Positive Preaching and the Modern Mind.* Grand Rapids: Baker, 1980.

Fox, Nili S. "Numbers." In *JSB* 281–355.

Friedrich, Gerhard. "κῆρυξ, κήρυγμα, κηρύσσω, κτλ.," in *TDNT* III:683–718.

Fretheim, Terence. *Exodus.* Interpretation: A Bible Commentary for Teaching and Preaching. Louisville: John Knox, 1997.

————. "Genesis." *NIB* I:321–674.

Furnish, Victor Paul. "Homosexuality." In *The Moral Teaching of Paul*, 52–82. Nashville: Abingdon, 1985.

Gagnon, Robert. *The Bible and Homosexual Practice*. Nashville: Abingdon, 2001.

———. "A Critique of Jacob Milgrom's Views on Leviticus 18:22 and 20:13." Online: http://www.robgagnon.net/articles/homoMilgrom.pdf.

Gaiser, Frederick J. "Homosexuality and the Old Testament." *WW* 10 (1990) 161–65.

———. "A New Word on Homosexuality?" Isaiah 56:1–8 as Case Study. *WW* 14 (1994) 280–293

———. "Preaching God: Hosea 11:1–11." *WW* 28 (2008) 203–9.

Gilthvedt, Gary. "Dying 'Through the Law to the Law' (Gal 2:19)." PhD diss., St. Andrews University, 1990. Online: http://www.ntgateway.com/paul-the-apostle/galatians/.

Gilthvedt, Mary Ronning. *If A Member Sins Against You: A Study of Matthew18:15–17*. MTh diss., Luther Seminary, 1997.

Goppelt, Leonhard. *Theology Of The New Testament*. Translated by John Alsup. Grand Rapids: Eerdmans, 1982.

Greenstein, Edward. "Exodus." In *HCSB* 77–150.

Hackett, Jo Ann. "Numbers." In *HCSB* 198–265.

———. "Violence and Women's Lives in the Book of Judges." *Interpretation* 58 (2004) 356–64.

Haenchen, Ernst. *The Acts Of The Apostles*. Translated by Bernard Noble, Gerald Shinn, and Hugh Anderson, Revised by R. McL. Wilson. Philadelphia: Westminster, 1965.

Harnack, Adolf von. *The Expansion of Christianity in the First Three Centuries*. Translated by James Moffatt. London: Williams and Norgate, 1904.

———. "The Social Question." In *What Is Christianity?* Translated by Thomas Saunders, 88–101. New York: Harper and Brothers, 1957.

Harper, Kyle. "*Porneia*: The Making of a Christian Sexual Norm." *JBL* 131 (2012), 363–83.

Hauck, Friedrich and Rudolf Meyer. "καθαρός, καθαρίζω, κτλ.," in *TDNT* III: 413–31.

Hauck, Friedrich and Siegfried Schulz. "πόρνη, πορνεύω, κτλ.," in *TDNT* VI:579–95.

Hay, David. "Pauline Theology After Paul." *Pauline Theology* IV:181–95. Atlanta: Scholars Press, 1997.

Hays, Richard B. *Echoes Of Scripture In The Letters Of Paul*. New Haven: Yale, 1989.

Hoad, John. "Some New Testament References to Isaiah 53." *ExpositoryTimes* 58 (1956) 254–55.

Hooker, Morna. "Beyond the Things that are Written? St. Paul's Use of Scripture." *NTS* 27 295–309.

———. "Interchange in Christ," *JTS* 22 (1971) 349–61.

# Bibliography

Hultgren, Arland. "Being Faithful to the Scriptures: Romans 1:26–27 as a Case in Point." *WW* XIV 315–25. Or see, www.ntgateway.com/paul-the -apostle/romans/.

———. *Paul's Letter to the Romans.* Grand Rapids: Eerdmans, 2011.

Hyatt, J. P. "Circumcision." *IDB* 1:629–31.

Jeremias, Joachim. "παῖς θεοῦ in Later Judaism in the Period after the LXX." In *TDNT* V:677–717.

Jewett, Robert. *Paul's Anthropological Terms.* Leiden: E. J. Brill, 1971.

Kaiser, Walter C., Jr. "Leviticus." *NIB* 1:983–1192.

Karlen, Arno. "The Greek Revision." In *Sexuality and Homosexuality: A New View.* New York: Norton, 1971.

———. "Homosexuality in History." In *Homosexual Behavior: A Modern Reappraisal.* New York: Basic, 1980.

Käsemann, Ernst. *Romans.* Translated and edited by Geoffrey Bromiley. Grand Rapids: Eerdmans, 1980.

Keck, Leander. "Romans." In *HCSB* 2114–2138.

Knust, Jennifer Wright. *Unprotected Texts.* New York: HarperCollins, 2011.

Kooy, V. H. "Hospitality." In *IDB* 2:654.

Köster, Helmut. "φύσις, κτλ.," in *TDNT* 9:251–77.

Lovelace, M. H. "Abomination." In *IDB* 1:12–13.

Luther, Martin. German Bible. In *BibleWorks5*.

———. *Lectures on Romans.* Translated and edited by Wilhelm Pauck. Phildelphia: Westminster, 1961.

Maccoby, Hyam. "Leviticus and Abomination." *Times Literary Supplement* 11 (1998) 17.

Mackay, John. *God's Order.* New York: Macmillan, 1953.

Malina, Bruce. *New Testament World: Insights from Cultural Anthropology.* Louisville: Westminster John Knox, 1991.

McKenzie, John L. *The World of the Judges.* Englewood Cliffs: Prentice–Hall, 1966.

Manson, T. W. "The Significance of Christ as Saviour." *On Paul and John,* 29–81. Naperville: Allenson, 1963.

Mendenhall, George. "Law and Covenant in the Ancient Near East." *The Biblical Archaeologist,* XVII.2:26–46, and 3:49–76.

Milgrom, Jacob. "Leviticus." In *HCSB* 151–97.

———. *Leviticus.*The Anchor Bible Commentary 3,3A,3B. New York: Doubleday, 2000.

Moule, C. F. D. "Death 'to Sin', 'to Law', and 'to the World': A Note on Certain Datives." 367–75. In *Mélanges Bibliques.* Gembloux, 1970.

Moulton, W. F. and A. S. Geden. *Concordance to the Greek Testament.* Edinburgh: T. & T. Clark, 1978.

Moxnes, Halvor. *Theology In Conflict.* Leiden: E. J. Brill, 1980.

Muilenburg, James. *The Way Of Israel.* New York: Harper, 1961.

Munck, Johannes. *Paul and the Salvation of Mankind.* Translated by Frank Clarke. London: SCM, 1959.

Myers, Jacob. *Judges*. Interpreter's Bible 2:809. New York, Abingdon: 1953.

Nanos, Mark D. "Romans." In *JANT* 353-86. New York: Oxford, 2011.

Neyrey, Jerome. *2 Peter, Jude*. The Anchor Bible 37. New York: Doubleday, 1993.

Nissinen, Martti. *Homoeroticism in The Biblical World*. Translated by Kirsi Stjerna. Minneapolis: Fortress, 1998.

Olson, Dennis T. "Judges." In *NIB* II:721-888.

Räisänen, Heikki. *Paul and the Law.*Tübingen: J. C. B. Mohr [Paul Siebeck], 1983.

Reicke, Bo. *The Epistles of James, Peter and Jude*. Anchor Bible 37.

Roetzel, Calvin. *The Letters of Paul*. Louisville: Westminster John Knox: 1998.

Rogers, Jack. *Jesus, the Bible, and Homosexuality*. Louisville: Westminster John Knox, 2006.

Rosenberg, Joel W. "Genesis." In *HCSB* 3-76.

Rylaarsdam, J. C. "Atonement." In *IDB* 1:309-16.

Sanders, E. P. *Paul, the Law, and the Jewish People*. Philadelphia: Fortress, 1983.

Scanzoni, Letha, and Virginia Ramey Mollenkott. *Is The Homosexual My Neighbor?* San Francisco: Harpers, 1978.

Scherer, Paul. *Love Is A Spendthrift*. New York: Harper & Brothers, 1961.

Schrenk, Gottlob. "δίκη, δικαιόω, κτλ.," in *TDNT* II:178-225.

Schwartz, Baruch J. "Leviticus." In *JSB* 203-80.

Schweitzer, Albert. *The Mysticism of Paul the Apostle*. London: Black, 1956.

Schweizer, Eduard. "Dying and Rising with Christ." *NTS* 14 (1968) 1-14.

Scroggs, Robin. *The New Testament and Homosexuality*. Philadelphia: Fortress, 1983.

Smith, Abraham. "*1 and 2 Thessalonians*." In *NOAB* 340-348.

Stählin, Gustav. "The Wrath of Man and the Wrath of God in the NT." *TDNT* V:419-47.

Stendahl, Krister. *The Bible and the Role of Women*. Translated by Emilie Sander. Philadelphia: Fortress, 1966.

Stewart, James S. *A Man in Christ*. Grand Rapids: Baker, 1975.

Tannehill, Robert. *Dying and Rising with Christ*. Berlin: Alfred Töpelmann, 1967.

Tiede, David. "Will Idolaters, Sodomizers, or the Greedy Inherit the Kingdom of God?" *A Pastoral Exposition of 1 Cor 6:9-10*. *WW* 10 (1990) 147-56.

Toombs, Lawrence. "Clean and Unclean." In *IDB* 1:641-54.

Traina, Robert. *Methodical Bible Study*. New York: Ganis & Harris, 1952.

Trible, Phyllis. "An Unnamed Woman: The Extravagance of Violence." In *Texts of Terror*, 65-91. Philadelphia: Fortress, 1984.

Von Rad, Gerhard. *Moses*. New York: Association, 1959.

———. *Old Testament Theology*. Translated by D.M.G. Stalker, 1:262-72. New York: Harper & Row, 1962.

Wallis, Jim. *God's Politics.*San Francisco: HarperCollins, 2005.

Wedderburn, A. J. M. *The Reasons For Romans*. Minneapolis: Fortress, 1991.

Westerholm, Stephen. *Israel's Law and the Church's Faith*. Grand Rapids: Eerdmans, 1988.

# Bibliography

Wills, Garry. *What Jesus Meant*. New York: Viking, 2006.

————. *What Paul Meant*. New York: Viking, 2006.

Wink, Walter. *Homosexuality and The Bible*. Pearl River: Ramapo, 2003.

Wright, G. Ernest. *God Who Acts*. London: SCM, 1962.

Wright, David . "Leviticus." In *NOAB* 142–83.

Ziesler, J. A. *The Meaning of Righteousness in Paul*. London: Cambridge, 1972.

Made in the USA
Las Vegas, NV
17 April 2021

21585288R10075